WILLIE CARSON
Up Front

WILLIE CARSON Up Front

A RACING AUTOBIOGRAPHY

Willie Carson and Brough Scott

STANLEY PAUL

LONDON

The authors and publishers would like to thank the following for allowing the use of copyright photographs:
BBC, Ed Byrne, Gerry Cranham, Hulton-Deutsch Collection, Press Association, Provincial Press Agency, *Racing Post*, Rex Features, Phil Smith, Sport & General, the *Sun*. Other photographs are from Willie Carson's personal albums.

First published 1993

1 3 5 7 10 8 6 4 2

© Willie Carson and Brough Scott 1993

Willie Carson and Brough Scott have asserted their right under the Copyright, Designs and Patents Act. 1988 to be identified as the authors of this work

First published in the United Kingdom in 1993 by
Stanley Paul & Co. Limited
Random House, 20 Vauxhall Bridge Road, London SW1V 2SA

Random House Australia (Pty) Limited
20 Alfred Street, Milsons Point, Sydney,
New South Wales 2061. Australia

Random House New Zealand Limited
18 Poland Road, Glenfield,
Auckland 10, New Zealand

Random House South Africa (Pty) Limited
PO Box 337, Bergvlei, South Africa

Random House UK Limited Reg. No. 954009

A CIP catalogue record for this book is available from the British Library

ISBN 0 09 174688 4

Printed in Great Britain by
Clays Ltd, St Ives plc

CONTENTS

INTRODUCTION

He now sits at the end of the rainbow: a little golden gnome who found a talent in his tinyness. It has been a long journey and there have been some bad bumps. But he has stuck to his craft and the game has kept him young, a fresh horse for every race. That, and what was there from the very beginning.

Because of the fitness, the jockey's frame and the single occupation in adulthood, it is not difficult to imagine the child from the man. Willie Carson at fifty is at times still an almost absurdly boyish figure. Watching him bustle around a race-course, five foot and seven and a half stone of crackling energy, is still to see May Carson's bairn hustling about Stirling back in the forties. You just accept that he discovered the beanstalk of riding success and presto, he was up there slaying giants, opening caves and stacking those crocks of gold into the back cupboard. Willie got his kingdom from the horse.

Of course it has been a lot more than pantomime. But the dynamos which drove him were always there: energy, fearless-ness and a certain cock-sparrow shrewdness which meant that he would never starve. Whilst it was a happy trick of fate which steered him towards the jockey's saddle, the only place where one of his size might prosper, it was Carson and only Carson who pushed, prodded and finally forced his way onto the racing stage. It was never easy. Neither, despite that cackling 'cheeky chappie' persona he adopted for TV interviews, is he.

He is comfortable enough. Home is a model modern Cotswold manor house just outside Cirencester looking across railed paddocks to where immaculate stud buildings rear new thoroughbreds for the market and the track, and where a cosy cottage repays proud parents for the early years when it was him under their wing.

Back in the house a couple of squabbling Jack Russell terriers are the only sign of disorder in the panelled kitchen, the plumped cushions and the sunlit conservatory where Elaine brings us coffee while we talk about the book. On the gravelled drive is a Mercedes, out beyond is a Piper Saratoga in which Carson wings about the country. He looks over half-moon glasses at photo collages of friends and, indeed, now of grand-children on the wall. He is friendly but not benign. He cannot be. He has to compete too much. It seems he always did.

This is his book, his story. My role is as your listener and guide. The words, the people, the anecdotes, whether they be right or wrong, painful or glorious, are something you must share direct.

It is a journey across Britain, from the working class of Stirling to Gloucestershire's horsey elite. But it is a journey much further afield, too. Willie has ridden all over the globe, has been in wars in India, in the ring with Ali, but most revealing is the voyage through time; our time, our place.

The same wee Scotsman has been through a grafting, but close-knit childhood. Through a Dickensian Yorkshire apprentice-ship, through push-bike and caravan days at Newmarket. Through the intoxication of success and the family casualties it brought. Through brutal accident and out into front-room fame. In the age of TV, Carson was the first and greatest communicator amongst the jockeys. Piggott may have been the distant genius. Willie was the champion you could understand. The little scuffler who made it all the way up to race for the Queen, and even, in the Nashwan saga, to tangle with her. Willie Carson's story is one for us all.   U

1
STIRLING

In one sense Stirling will never change. Not as long as the Castle stands and the river runs. The old boast of 'Gateway to the Highlands' may be inexact, but for anyone in the city the look remains up and out.

The rock of Stirling is a slab of granite put there by the Ice Age and by a creator who must have known its effect down the ages. From its castle, Scots would have peered south to see the English trekking those last ten miles from Falkirk and remembered the triumph that was Robert Bruce's at Bannockburn. When England ruled, anxious eyes would have scanned north to Dunblane to see if the clans were gathering on the road to Perth. That was all in the past. Long before Billy Carson.

Yes, only the English called him Willie. Stirling was a Protestant town, the boys there historically support Glasgow Rangers rather than Celtic, the Catholic team. Billy was a Protestant name. You knew where you were. In November 1942 May Carson was admitted to Stirling hospital for the baby, her first born, to arrive. Home was a two-roomed flat in Windsor Cottages. Tommy Carson worked for Fyffes, the banana people, and was waiting for call-up. There were no riches around. Not of the material kind anyway.

Looking down from the Castle today, you can see shopping precincts, super stores, factory sites, even one of Her Majesty's more modern prisons. In 1942 the prospects were much bleaker, more cramped, at least from the urban view. But what is clear even now is how near the country is. The mighty Forth still snakes its great river arms around the east of the city. Out beyond it in winter the snow sits atop Ben Cleuch. Much closer by, sheep and a couple of ponies still graze in the meadows next to the ruined Cambuskenneth Abbey, the same meadows where young Billy's grandad kept pigs, trotters, greyhounds and the rest.

Billy may not have been born to privilege, his path must have seemed a million miles from the blue-blooded thoroughbreds with which he would later carve his own little niche in sporting history, but the Carson upbringing was clearly strong on both love and freedom. 'Everyone used to say what a wonderful look-ing wee boy he was,' remembers May Carson, still spry, alert and mother-bird caring in her late seventies. 'We didn't have any money but we always had food and he was always so neat and tidy. I used to go off to work but he could always look after him-self.'

The son will snort at the mothering. The tick will go in his cheek and he will laugh: 'Well, nearly always. I was an indepen-dent little sod.' Being as unsentimental as he is, Willie Carson is not in the habit of returning to his birthplace. But you will find much of the spirit and toughness that was 'Billy' remains. Once again Stirling has left its mark.   U

The Carsons were immigrants from Northern Ireland. My father lost both his parents when he was seven, so he never had any real recollection of them.

One of my first memories was when my father went away to the war. I remember looking out from a window down at Stainers Abbey. My parents lodged, I think, with a Mrs Toyle when they first got married. They had a room upstairs with a window that looked straight down to the little bridge at the Northern Court. I remember that my father had a cap and he was waving it as he walked away. He had a pack on his back, not one of those great big jobs, just a small one.

It was 1944, so I was only two, but I remember the bombers going over. They dropped a few on us. Both things – father going off and the bombs falling – would account for my mother being upset. I remember the humming of the bombers. Every night they kept going over and kept dropping bombs. I think the house across the road from us was hit. I was thirty, forty feet away. I don't remember being afraid, all I remember is hearing the sound of the bombers and then the bang. My mother hid me under the table, I think. It was a traumatic experience for her and I suppose it got through to me.

My father was a Royal Engineer, a mine detector. He went over on D-Day with the commandos. He landed somewhere near Caen, looked down at this village near the coast and saw it was absolutely swarming with Germans. He was never hit by bullets. The closest he got was one day when the washing was on the line and a plane came down and started firing. He ran like hell for the trench. When he went back for his washing his vest had bloody great bullet holes in it. He wrapped it up and took it home. When my mother saw it she screamed, 'You weren't in it, were you?'!

I don't know where my mother's family, the Hunters, come from. My old grandfather, though, was a bit of a lad. In his younger days he was in County Durham, where he married his second wife, my step-grandmother. He was a pit-head manager – and a rebel, an Arthur Scargill. He was always for the workers, wanting more money, wanting the lads to fight. I heard that he was once in so much trouble that he stuck all his furniture in a van and sent it back to Scotland. When I first remember him, he had just retired from managing a pit near Stirling.

He was a bit of a boxing promoter as well. My mother has the stool that he used to have in the corner. He once promoted a fight with the guy who had a bear called Hercules up in Kirk.

Grandfather lived by the Abbey. I used to play there a lot on my own. He had everything: greyhounds, pigeons, chickens, sheep, a couple of pigs. There was always something happening, and in his orchard there was always something to eat.

I remember playing outside my grandfather's after dark. Outside his gates seemed to be the meeting place for all the local boys. It was a dead-end place, never any traffic, and at the end of the row of houses we used to play with coins: heads and tails, pitch and toss. I used to gamble a bit. When we got hungry, we went to a bakery round the corner. We always had two to go and buy buns and the other lot used to fill their pockets up with cakes. The baker must have rumbled us but we were never nicked.

As a kid I didn't get on with my step-grandmother. If grandfather wasn't there when I went into the house, I'd get out quick, because if you did anything wrong, she was always at you.

My sister, Elizabeth, was born four years after me. I first remember her being in the bathroom and my mother getting all excited about the black and blue marks. She was a year or so old when she started suffering from TB. My mother was terribly upset. She had had TB herself, before I was five. She went to a sanatorium in Edinburgh for six months and I stayed with my father's aunt, who had brought my father up after he was orphaned. I called her granny. I had a three-wheeler bike, and I remember going flat out down a steep hill into the main road and under a bus. I wasn't hurt, but I was frogmarched up to granny and she gave me a right rollocking.

Granny lived in a place called Alva, five miles from Stirling. She had an upstairs flat looking down onto a biggish garden and with a main road running along the bottom. A cherry tree clogged up the side of the house, which was cream coloured. Across the road was the Co-op grocery shop and a little lane. There was a group of about four shops down there with stairs on the outside that went up to granny's flat.

My sister was in hospital on and off for eight years. She was always going in – once, twice a week, sometimes for longer periods. She was the first person in Stirling to have Streptomycin injections. When she came out of hospital she was very delicate but I remember I wasn't that delicate with her. If she went on, I just thumped her. She said I was jealous of her. I don't recall that but of course I was spoilt and when she came back again, I felt a bit pushed out.

As a kid I never sat around at all. After school, I'd be straight out in the park or in a field playing football. I was always outside.

On my fifth birthday I remember I was running around the corner of this cottage – I don't know what I was doing there – and I slipped and fell in the river. I think I got stuck in the mud. Someone came and got me out. I was screaming. I nearly drowned. It was always said that I nearly drowned three times. I don't really remember the first time. My mother must have told me about it. There was a copper boiler engine sunk in the ground for water for the ducks. It was about three feet deep, maybe more, and I fell in it. But I somehow got myself out.

The third time was later on. I remember I was really panicky. Two people lost their lives in the Forth every year around the Stirling area. Some folk used to go swimming there because we didn't have any swimming baths. I couldn't swim so I'd just walk about and on one occasion there was a hole in the ground. I got out of it, though.

When I was about seven we lived at 5 Grampian Street, a pre-fab, just round the corner from 73 Churchill Avenue, the first house my parents ever had. We were there for five years. There was a woman who lived on the main road who had a TV set and we all went in and watched Muffin the Mule. It was fantastic, really exciting. We'd never had a TV set.

I was always tiny – I had been a small baby, only six and a half pounds. Grandfather on my mother's side wasn't very big either, though I don't know about the other relatives. When I was about six or seven I was always being picked on. Ray Hackston, who lived across the road, was always bloody well picking. I used to go home crying and father used to go out and stick up for me. But he got fed up with that, so he bought me some boxing gloves and taught me how to box. He roughed me up a bit trying to teach me how to look after myself. Over the years I became quite clever at running. Somehow you learn how to get out of things and how to tell people to piss off.

I went to Riverside Primary School. I'd bike it there – I went everywhere on my bike. At school we always got the impression that the English looked after themselves before they gave us anything. (It was true: Scotland never had a motorway until a lot later.) And Protestants and Catholics was a big thing. It was them and us. They had their own school and went on a different bus. We were always segregated, whatever we did. After school all the kids played in the park. I was a Protestant and we were always arguing about whose side we'd be on if we were all Protestants. But then, if a big load of Catholics turned up, we'd play them. We knew straight away that they were Catholics because they wore different school ties and scarves and had their own colours.

On my estate, I don't know how it happened, but you'd get a few Catholic houses together and then it would be mostly

Protestants. We used to throw stones through their windows. If you could get up to any mischief it would be against them. They weren't enemies though.

We only went to church on special occasions. In those days they had something like poppy days. Father always went to the Cenotaph for the parade for the dead. And all the small villages had their little parades and a service with a cross.

I spent a lot of time going to see Elizabeth in hospital and also going with father to the warehouse. He only ever had one job in his life, with Fyffes bananas. He started around eight o'clock and was back around half five. He must have been made foreman quite early, because he had to go on Saturdays or Sundays to check the rooms and fill them up with methylene gas to ripen the bananas. Wagons would come in right by the railway side to be unloaded and the bananas, all in bunches, were like rocks. Sometimes I'd go along to work with him. I used to help, doing a bit of sticking labels on. I think we used to go to the warehouse on the bus though father always used a bicycle. Even later when he had a car he used a bike and mother had the car.

He takes his politics quite seriously now, but he didn't seem to in those days. He won't tell me how he votes. To talk to him you'd think he was Labour but I think he has been Conservative for a good many years. He was never a member of a union.

After primary school I went to the Territorial for two years. The Territorial was not far away in Union Street. You went from Stirling Primary to the Territorial and then you moved up to the Allen High School on Upper Castle Hill. I don't remember much about the second school, except that I sat beside Helen Bick, who married Billy Bremner.

After I was twelve I started jumping school – I just didn't bother turning up. I got someone to write a note for me and I went down to the cattle market and got sixpence for moving the cattle around from pen to pen. I'd spend it on sweets. There was another cattle market where I never went except in daylight. That was no-go land: all the rough lot, the drunkards, were down there. They had fights and if they didn't like you, they threw you over the balcony.

I didn't really have any one mate. I had friends, but there wasn't one who stood out from the others. I was always too busy to have a mate.

I had a paper round with a Mr Hogg, who had a shop opposite the Territorial School on Douglas Street. I must have been about eleven when I started and I did the round for about five years. I don't recall him but there was a woman who sort of ran the shop. She was up at six every morning. I got to know all the characters in the town, all the scruffy ones, all the paper people and the paper boys. There was one guy, a scruffy old bugger with one leg. I used to go and have a chat with him. His face was never clean, he never washed and there he'd be in bed with his leg lying on the floor.

Over the bridge, that was a run nobody wanted to take because it was such a long way. It used to take me an hour and a half every morning, seven days a week. I used to hate Sundays, going round with my bag. I used to struggle a bit. Then I found a way of doing it: I'd sling the bag on the handlebars and bike along.

I used to be out of the house first and got back when everybody had left. Sometimes I'd stay for a cup of tea, then go to school. When I came home from school, father used to come back for lunch. Mother would leave something and I'd heat it up. I used to cook for him, get his tea ready. I was quite interested in cooking. My mother got me into it. I used to do bacon and ham pies. I could cook quite well – still could if I put my mind to it.

At night-time I used to go from school to the railway station, pick up all the evening papers from the train from Glasgow, take them to the paper shop and start my evening run. They must have trusted me to give me that job.

I used to get ten and sixpence a week for the round and a bit extra for collecting papers at night. I gave the ten and sixpence to my mother. She was working as a waitress in the Fourways restaurant in Dunn Lane. I think she went off about nine o'clock and got back about seven at night.

Occasionally I used to throw the papers, but we'd get into trouble when you could put them through the letter box.

Anybody who didn't give you tips would get their papers slung though. I collected money for tips once a week. That was always an extra two hours, knocking on doors and getting the money. I got more money out of tips than I did wages. I always had a couple of coppers in my pocket and could buy a bar of chocolate whenever I wanted. I got the better of my mother on this. I said to her, 'Here's my first wage packet, mum. What do you want, the wage packet or the tips?' She took the wage packet and I smiled because the tips were bigger.

I joined the Life Boys. They were similar to the Boy Scouts, which I didn't fancy somehow. They wore blue and had hats and used to march. I got fed up after about a year. Then somebody took my cap and I don't think I went back after that.

I knocked around a lot, played football or made conkers, did the normal things that other boys did. You always wanted the conkers that were in the trees. You couldn't wait for them. I'd throw sticks up to knock them down and get into trouble: 'Get out of here, you bastards!'. I used to go in the bushes in Park Drive to smoke. I went nicking apples and used to throw a few bangers into letter boxes. And we'd get a roll of cotton and after dark tie it onto a doorknocker, go across the road, and knock, knock, knock on the door. Someone would come out. Great fun. Then you'd run.

We played football in King's Park. I used to take my soccer quite seriously. Typical Scots kid. I always wanted to be a football player. I played plenty of football but I was never a star. My father was quite good – he was brought up with it and played for the Army and for Alva and Alloa.

I bought a record player and used to buy my own records. I loved instrumental, Chuck Berry's early stuff, Elvis Presley, the Big Bopper and John Delight. The record shop was just up from my father's.

I remember trying to get away with a girl who lived on my paper round. They had a big house, with a big car and a pony. I caught her eye a few times and I kept saying hello and hanging around. And then I saw her when I was out cycling one day and I saw quite a bit of her after that. But I remember thinking to myself that she was way above me. I was definitely working class. I didn't feel any anger or think there was anything wrong in it. I just thought they were lucky.

I left school when I was fifteen, in 1957. I remember Allen High School only vaguely. I wasn't interested in school: I could tell I wasn't going to be Prime Minister. I did finish third in a class once and got a new bike from my dad for it.

In my teens we sometimes had day trips up to Aberdour by the sea. We borrowed a car off grandfather. He had a big Morris Oxford 16, a mafia job with tail boards and huge lights. I remember the windows were all a bit cracked and were glued together.

Grandfather was quite a player. He always had money in his pocket. I went in the woods with him playing cards. They'd have a hundred quid on a card. It was illegal so they had look-outs all over the place. His face never changed, he could play poker. He was a well-known character of Stirling in his day. He seemed to know everybody. He was an interesting man, always kept me amused telling me why he was doing things, always going to the market, always dealing, always trying to buy or sell something. I learned how to do a few things through him, like getting a fish out of the water by tickling it and then taking it straight up to the fishmongers.

Grandfather had a bike with a basket on the front. He'd go to buy stale bread for the greyhounds and I used to take them for a walk. I never had a dog or a cat. The only animals I ever kept were rabbits. I always had one in a hutch in the back garden and used to feed and look after it. Grandfather's greyhounds always ran away with me. They were mostly his own, though sometimes he had a share with other people. They were raced at a track in Falkirk but I never went there. Grandfather was never involved with the police – but the coppers were the baddies.

We went to Edinburgh once in grandfather's car. My Auntie Mary lived in a street that was all tenements. By the time we got to her house the kids were climbing all over the car. They thought it was a wedding: in those days the bride and groom used to throw pennies out of the car window and whenever there was a wedding there were always a hundred kids waiting for their pennies.

It was a rough place, about the worst in Britain. There were gang wars, fights, even occasional deaths. It was all in the newspapers, on the radio. I'd never been to London, so going into Edinburgh, the city, down the Royal Mile, was like going to Mars.

The cinema became important to me. You could say it changed my life. There were three cinemas in Stirling. On Saturday mornings I always used to go down to the Regal, next to the railway station and the cattle market. They showed Dan Dare: 'To be continued next week. . .'. I believe I was eleven when I saw *The Rainbow Jacket*, with Teddy Underdown, who died recently, as the trainer and Robert Morley. The jock turned out to be six foot two. His mother wrote to me about ten years ago.

I had never sat on a horse except for an old trotter at my grandfather's. It was standing at the gate and I jumped on it. My memory says that it went flat out (I should think it trotted) through the trees. When it got to the iron railings I got off and I can remember saying, 'I ain't going to do that again.' But people would say 'Billy, ooh aren't you light, you ought to be a jockey' and then I saw *The Rainbow Jacket* and it made a big impression. I thought, 'Yeah, he did well, that fellah out there, got all the glory and money.' So I never bothered much with schooling. I didn't have to do too much to be a jockey: all you do is sit on a horse. All the other people swot but, I thought, I won't have to use my brain. I didn't worry about actually learning to ride.

I started riding when I was about twelve. I didn't like going to the riding school, though. I used to cycle seven miles and change in the café by the school. I felt very embarrassed wearing those breeches. I was the only boy and I couldn't ride for toffee. One horse went off with me very fast and I just slipped down the side. I found it very hard. It didn't come easily like riding a bike. Mrs MacGregor was trying to teach me to do riding-school style: heels down and straight back.

I quite liked being around the ponies, but I didn't feel as though I belonged. I always felt an outsider. In my day a working-class kid going into these riding schools was unheard of. The others' mums and dads were all toffs, all business people with cars and detached houses. The kids all had yellow polo-neck sweaters.

My mother paid for the riding lessons with the money I made from my paper round. It seemed a waste but I was a determined little bugger. Like the paper round that nobody else would do, I was determined I would do it.

2
MIDDLEHAM

What a journey! Even today the 250 miles from Stirling to Middleham seems an interminable drag all down the right-hand shoulder of the country. Back in the blizzard-hit January of 1958 it must have seemed like crossing the Pole. Tommy and May and Billy bumping down for Billy to start his life in stables. In every sense he was off to another country.

Through Edinburgh, past Dunbar, then on that coast road all the way through Berwick and past Holy Island you go. Then inland a little, past Alnwick and Morpeth to reach Newcastle and Durham. That's where you pick up the motorway now. It says something for how far back we have gone that Britain's first motorway didn't come until December 1958 – and that only an eight-mile stretch of the Preston by-pass.

Jet flights to America began that winter, too. But for the occupants of the little car pushing on across the North Yorkshire plain from Darlington and taking the spectacular gorge road from Richmond beside the River Swale, such thoughts were about as likely as putting their tiny son in outer space. It was to be another three years before the Russians sent Yuri Gagarin on that opening circuit of the heavens. Quite a bit longer before anyone thought that W. Carson was worth shuttling across the Atlantic and beyond to ride a horse. At this stage he could hardly hold a broom.

Maybe he was already streetwise enough to have negotiated that 'tips or wage packet' deal with his mother, but he was just fifteen, fair haired, blue eyed and angel faced. What were his parents letting him in for? They were trying to give him a chance. At least, however unfamiliar, however unlikely the odds of success, it was something their boy wanted to try.

Leyburn now is a storybook market town in the Dales straight from the pages of James Herriot, with many of the knick-knacks and memorabilia to match. A couple of miles away Middleham stands proud at the foot of the Moor. Over a fence a giant, twelve-wheel horsebox gleams impressively under the light. To the left Richard III's ruined castle evokes the past. Out of the village and before taking the other mile to where the forbidding face of Thorngill Stables sits above on the bank, you can see a modern all-weather gallop climbing up the hill to the right, whilst below it lie the weeds and water of Pinkers Pond, a landmark whose name is to ring in this story.

In January 1958 Billy Carson was going to a different universe all right. It was one of earth and hooves and straw. ∪

We had had letters back from all three racing trainers I had written to asking for trials. I remember my mother saying I had to make up my mind. We had discussed it before, and I kept fobbing her off. Then I said, 'Oh. . . Armstrong.' And that's how I came to go to Gerald Armstrong.

I didn't know anything else about racing but I did take a bit of an interest in the statistics of what was going on. I didn't go to George Boyd because no-one ever makes it in Scotland. And I never thought about Newmarket: it didn't enter my head. So it was going to be between Beasley and Armstrong. I chose Armstrong because he had a bit of a reputation for having good apprentices.

My father had always had a bet. He was a six shilling lad. My grandfather never backed a horse in his life. He'd have £500 on a greyhound, but he didn't trust the jocks. I didn't bet either and I don't recall ever getting a paper and looking to see what had won a race, or listening to the racing on radio.

The desire to be a jockey was kindled when I was in Sunderland for the holidays and we went to Newcastle to see the racing. We brought the car up on the inside of the course. My only recollection of that day was standing by the rail and the horses thundering by. Bloody hell, didn't they go fast? I said, 'Cor, I'll be able to do that one day.' I can still see one jockey's face, his roundish cheeks and the determination in his eyes. The excitement, the speed, shone through. There wasn't any fear. I had no reason, at that age, to be frightened, though the horses did seem gigantic.

The move to Middleham was eventful in itself. Going there was a nightmare. It was January 1958, quite early in the morning, and we had to follow a snow-plough. We were in our own car, a Morris Minor, the first my father ever owned. He drove me down, with mum, and I remember the snow either side of the road – it was like the Cresta run. And when we got there, oh my God, it was a bleak-looking place. When they showed us where I was going to live my mother didn't want to leave me. There was a dormitory, no carpets, stone floors, no curtains, an army bed and a blanket. I wouldn't say that I was a totally clean boy but I was quite tidy and I felt this was dirty.

Gerald Armstrong seemed all right though. He looked a whizzo old man really when I first met him. My parents stayed for a while. I cried the day after they left. I had known that if I was a success I was going to be away – I'd had plenty of time to think about it – but I always thought I'd be going home from the training. I was just turned fifteen and I didn't realise at the time that I wouldn't see my parents again for the best part of a year. I'm not a great writer, but I was so homesick the letters went flowing off every day, telling them how much I missed them and that I wasn't having a good time.

The first morning I was just shown what to do. You got into it much more gradually than you do now. Being taught how to sweep was the first job. It was a month before I started on my first horse. It was like being at riding school. You were virtually fags, cleaning the boots and washing shirts for the older lads. You had to do it all. And then you got put in cold baths. I had to run around the house, with nothing on, on cobble stones. I was often near to quitting during the first few years.

The winter of 1962 was the worst. We've not had one as bad since. I kept my pyjamas on for two whole months. I suppose it was sheer determination that kept me going. I kept saying, 'I'll give it just a bit longer...' I was paid two and sixpence a week compared with ten and six plus tips as a paper boy.

The food was pretty basic. The hatches would open and the plates came flying through. I don't recall what we had, but there was always plenty of sponge pudding with custard at the end of it. We had a cook, Bill, who was queer, and in a way he looked after us.

The lads all lived together. One of the older ones was nineteen or twenty and he was king of the castle. Right little bastard, he was. I said to John Forbes recently, 'What would you do with him if you caught him now?' and he said he'd kill him. I feel the same. He is one of the few men I could do the dirty on. He was evil, a Hitler, he absolutely terrorised us. He used to seem a big guy, but he was only about five foot one. I've no idea if he's still about now. I hope he's dead.

Three of us – me, John 'Jumbo' Forbes and Dougy Armstrong – became pals, so there was some protection. Dougy came from Wooler in the Borders. He was a sheep farmer, a big, strong lad, though quite soft in a way. He's the head of the gas board shop in Redcar now. John Forbes came from Saltburn. He was a great talker and became a salesman. He went into all sorts of things. He left us and went across the road to Hartingdon, to try to flog a few jumpers. He has his own company now, Forbes Ambrow. He's very successful in computers. The three of us were together for four or five years and we are still quite close today.

We worked seven days a week. We'd start at about seven. We didn't get any tea in the morning and if you wanted something to eat you'd put bread and jam under your pillow and sleep on it.

In the morning we mucked out all the horses and then rode out first lot. It would take an hour and a half I suppose. Then it would be breakfast. It was never straight out of the pans – it would have been ready for the last hour. After breakfast we'd ride out second lot. That's never as exciting as first lot, because there's less happening. Riding work, we used to go down the road and back up to the low moor. The road was pretty empty in those days and everyone slowed down for us. I quite enjoyed being on the moors. I would go nicking eggs. We caught a duck one day and tried to barbecue it, very unsuccessfully. We used to try to cook chips on the shovel.

After riding second lot I used to sweep up the yards and clean the tack. We only had two horses each to do in those days. Some people only had one – I did in the first year. Staff were very cheap then and the place was full of apprentices rather than paid lads.

We used to take turns looking after the copper, each doing it about twice a week. You had to look after it all afternoon: stoking it up and keeping the fire going. I used to get it stoked well up and then get a few bran sacks and fall asleep in front of the fire. It was good. And then in the evening it was brushing the horses over.

We ran everywhere. We used to race and over short distances I always used to get left. When we finished work, it was a couple of hundred yards from the yard up to the dormitory and I was always third. But when we ran from home to Middleham, about two miles, I started to come into my own.

We never had much money. We went to the pictures once a week, used to run twice a week. For a time I would go to Leyburn to see a bird every night. I used to run there and back, five miles the round trip. A little girl resulted from that. When the baby came, I panicked and dropped her. She's married now with two children.

I was still fifteen when I got drunk for the first time. I got caught as well. I drank two bottles of Newcastle Amber in Leyburn. Somebody paid for it and gave it to us and we drank it outside the pub. Suddenly I didn't feel well and I wanted to get home. It was dark by the time I set off and I was on my own. Every time a car came along I'd dive into a ditch, thinking it would be the cops. Then I thought, to hell with it, I'm not diving in the ditch again. And the very next car that came *was* the cops. They put me in the back and took me home. I gave them the wrong name and the wrong stable. They set me out and as they drove away I went as if to walk into the stable. When they had gone I went back down the hill and home. I believe they went to that stable the next day looking for me.

After that I used to go to the pub often – too often, I suppose, but there was nothing much to do at the stables except a bit of soccer. I remember getting pissed a few times. The guy who worked on the farm had a van and he'd chuck us in the back and take us home.

The only other place we went at night in Middleham was the café. We had egg sandwiches and played the pinball machine and listened to records. There was a dance once a week or so in the hall where they had the cinema. Invariably it all ended up in fights. I didn't get involved. I used to throw a punch and leave quick.

At one time Jumbo had a car and we used to go to the dance halls in Darlington, about twenty-six miles away. Coming back one night we had three punctures. We had to abandon the car and start walking to get back for work. We walked down the A1 towards Catterick Bridge, got a lift for a few miles, then started walking through Catterick Camp. We ran two telegraph poles, walked the next one, ran two, all the way home.

I don't think I had a holiday before Christmas 1958. Fred Astor, the head man, and Charlie Brown, a box driver who was always very helpful to us, looked after all the horses from 22 December until just after the New Year. The horses stayed in their boxes and were hayed, watered and fed for those two weeks while everybody, the whole staff, went home for the holidays. I went back to Stirling on the train. It was great going home: a long journey but fantastic.

Gerald Armstrong was a forgetful fellah – but he was a nice old boy. He would creep up and tip you out of bed if you were sleeping in the afternoon. One of my jobs was as coal boy. I got another shilling a week for filling up all the buckets in Gerald's house. We were allowed one bucket of coke a day. One day, when we were freezing, Dougy, Jumbo and I lifted the coal shed door off its hinges so that we could get some coal to warm ourselves up. We were just getting it into the bucket when we saw a light and heard someone coming. It was Gerald. We got into the coal shed and closed the door, but he could see our feet. The next day he called the coppers in to give us a talking to in the office, to frighten us so that we didn't do it again.

In the end I became his handyman. I used to get paid extra for painting windows and doors and I earned a shilling an hour for haymaking in the afternoons – pretty good compared to what we were getting a week.

Sometimes in the afternoon Gerald would get us on the sacks in the feed house, a wooden shed where he kept the corn. He'd stick a bridle on the end of a sack and have us changing hands and practising coping with horses changing legs. He did that with all the lads who were going to ride – there were three or four of us. When Ted Larkin was an apprentice, Gerald's father, Bob Armstrong, had him doing that. Once, when he got tired with the pushing, Bob said, 'Why have you stopped pushing, boy?' and Ted, a fast lad, said, 'I'm giving him a breather round the turn, sir.'

Ted was our big hero. 'Ted Larkin's coming to work tomorrow,' we'd say, and whoever went up with him would watch him ride and work, and then we'd sit down and discuss what he did: when he changed his hands, and pulled his stick through. He did it so quickly you couldn't see.

I started riding work when I was sixteen on a horse called Dentifrice. He was just an ordinary animal and probably didn't pull a lot but it felt to me as if he was running away. I weighed about six stone twelve pounds. The first horse I ever looked after was called Marija. She was a silly old cow: wanted to kill you and used to kick all the time. In the old days they made horses that way. But of course I got fond of her. Another one I remember was Taxanatania. He was savage – he was supposed to have killed someone back in Ireland. I looked after him for a while until he became too much for me. He was the sort that had to be put on two chains. He'd stand up against the wall of his box waiting for you to come at him. He was a bastard. I don't think he ever saw a racecourse. My parents were there when he arrived – they used to come down a lot. I bent down to get a bit of grass and Taxanatania started savaging me. Father had to chase him off.

I didn't feel as though I was making much progress, although I probably was. Nothing at that time was easy and everything I rode was always running away with me. Dougy was a strong lad and John Forbes a very determined fellah. He actually got to ride before I did. He was more mature and might have been a bit better than me. I was quite a slow learner.

It was a disgrace to fall off at Gerald Armstrong's. People didn't really get hurt that much, it was the disgrace of falling off in front of the other lads that was the biggest thing. We all knew which were the horses that were hard to sit on and although as kids we were never put on them, eventually we were and we all wondered how we were going to stay on. It was all nerves. If you didn't fall off, you'd be so relieved.

I remember some of Sam Armstrong's apprentices coming up and we couldn't believe it. Eddie Kinshaw was wearing a suit and had his own stick. We used to wear jeans, wellies and a cap – no crash helmet. We were allowed two pairs of jeans and two pairs of wellies a year and I think we had waterproofs in the winter. There was no hot water at our place and I think I bathed once a month. We had one lad who never washed. He had blue legs from the jeans. He once wanted time off to go home so he chopped the end off one of his fingers, picked the bit up and went to see the Captain. He came from Leeds and was thick.

There was this evil older lad, a horrible little git. He used to rob us. My parents were always sending us parcels and we'd hide them in a suitcase under our beds. But he knew when we had one and would break into the case and pinch it. We never got anything. He organised boxing some nights, upstairs in the dormitory. He'd move all the beds back and make a boxing ring on the bare boards. There were about a dozen lads and he'd just pick us out: you fight him, you fight him, and so on. Dougy knocked seven barrels out of one of them. It was bare knuckles, there was blood everywhere. When it came to my turn I had to fight the lunatic, the second-eldest lad there. I thought, right, mate, I'm going to kill you. I threw a punch but he ducked and hit me and of course down I went. That was my boxing career.

Fred Astor, the head lad, had a car, though he never used to go to work in it. I suppose he couldn't afford the petrol. I used to back it out of the garage and drive it up and down the drive. He never knew. I passed my driving test the first time of asking, a week after my seventeenth birthday in my father's car in Northallerton. I'd had quite a bit of experience, though I didn't exactly go for lessons: it was more a case of nicking a car and belting along the lanes round Middleham. The examiner was very interested in horses and we sat behind some traffic lights talking about a horse I looked after that he had backed.

I didn't have my own car for ages. I still had to hitch lifts to get about. You could hitch quite easily in those days. People were marvellous. If two cars went by, you could nearly always guarantee that the third one would stop for you.

3
REDCAR AND
ONWARDS

It's the most important watershed of them all. It's what every kid who goes into stables dreams about. They may be heavy, talentless or afraid for their lives, but if it's happened it's graduation time. They have donned the jockey's silks. Even if only once, they have had 'a ride' in public.

The very phrase is significant. The question 'how many rides have you had?' only ever pertains to racetrack performance. No matter that the youth or girl in question has ridden all sorts of racehorses of a morning for the full stretch of their working lives, they have still 'never had a ride'. It's only the racecourse that counts.

Even if well disguised beneath an obviously unskilful exterior, the compulsion can be huge. Sam was a friend of mine. He was a small, squatly made Yorkshireman who could shift buckets and muck out boxes better than any lad around. What he couldn't do with any sort of finesse was to make a racehorse go quicker. His obvious career path was up through the stable routines to taking charge of a yard. No-one considered giving him a ride as a jockey. So he left for Scandinavia. He didn't stay more than a couple of years but he rode in plenty of races. He came back to yard work but he had had his moments – in the Norwegian sun.

You never forget the first ride. Every moment of that day, every second in the saddle will be etched deep into the memory. So much has been invested for this. Not just your own energy but the support and belief of family, friends, schoolteachers, even of that man in the pub who lent you a fiver. It's the mysterious world which first intoxicated you all those years ago and now you are actually going to be in it. It's as if you are holding your breath for the whole afternoon.

You will see them every week. Young kids with faces made old by apprehension. It's their first time. It could be the beginning of something big. Far more often it's actually an excitement never to be bettered. Very rarely could you guess that you are seeing a name that will make it in the history books. Not one man in a million would have done that at Redcar in May of 1959.

But he did. From little acorns great oaks do spring. ♘

I had my first ride in 1959 on Marija. It was an apprentice handicap at the Whitsunside meeting at Redcar on Monday, 18 May. I was known as W.H. Carson in those days. I only had six stone eleven pounds to carry, though I don't recall it being any problem. I finished last.

There were six runners but the one that should have won was left at the start and took no part. The race was over a straight seven furlongs. I walked the course beforehand and I remember Gerald saying, 'It's a straight course, so fix your eye on something like a church spire and make your line for it so that you keep straight.' I don't think about it now, but keeping a horse straight isn't easy and I went from one side of the track to the other. The church spire moved. I got a real bollocking for not keeping straight. And Charlie Brown talked to me for hours about it, telling me that I should have fixed my eye on something.

I remember going away absolutely shaking in my boots. A terrible feeling. It was excitement, but there was a lot of nervous fear, too, just to see one's jockey heroes. I didn't have any kit of my own, I had to borrow it. The valets were the ones who told you what to do.

I was very disappointed. I only rode Marija because she was my filly and it was the end of the road for her. They were hoping that she would do something. She'd won as a two-year-old but at three she hadn't done much – down the field at Catterick Bridge under Norman McIntosh, and at Ripon under Ted Larkin. She ended up in South Africa. Best place for her.

I was coming up to seventeen and deep down I knew that I wasn't very good. I wasn't learning quickly enough. Now I ride any horse I want to whereas then I was frightened to death because there were certain horses in the yard I couldn't ride. I knew I wasn't ready. The more mature, stronger boys were doing better than me. I don't think Dougy got many rides but John Forbes had a few.

Red Cockade was the only other ride I had that year. It was an outsider at Catterick Bridge. We finished last. John Forbes had earlier finished third on it at Ripon and I had been a bit disappointed not to ride it that day.

My parents were very supportive when I went home for Christmas that year. They always told me to keep at it, not to get disappointed. They were very, very good.

I didn't have any winners in 1960 or 1961. I had twenty-two rides before the first winner. I remember asking for a ride of Jack Fawcus's that was a fruit and nut case nobody else would ride. It ran away with everybody and you couldn't pull it up. It didn't bolt and go flat out, it bolted slowly and when you came to stop, it just kept going at the same pace. Even Jumbo Wilkinson, a great jockey then, couldn't hold it. I rode it two or three times, once at Worcester over six furlongs. There was a big entrance with wrought iron gates at the end of the track with one rail across. The gate had an ornate bolt, which was lucky, because it just made the horse stick his toes in and spin round. I rode the horse at Haydock, too. I always had to hack it down to the start first or last. In the race it didn't matter, because it never went as fast as the others.

We didn't have a great many winners in Gerald's yard: we were always just scraping into the teens. Cascais ran every week and kept winning. Every time the horsebox started up he started to shake. He knew where he was going.

I often thought about quitting. When I was eighteen I virtually asked for a job in the Cow and Gate cheese factory at the bottom of the hill in Middleham. I kept thinking I might work in a chippy, be a chef. We used to get together with the lads from the cheese factory and compared to us they were making big money. They could afford packets of cigarettes and go out to the pub and drink and eat what they wanted.

I felt I was in the wrong place at Armstrong's. People kept saying, it's no good going there because there are too many good boys but I was always competitive and I could see that I had a better chance than most of the others because of my stature. It was about this time that Harry Moore, who trained at Doncaster, offered money for me. He liked the way I rode, even though I hadn't had any winners, and offered five hundred quid for my indentures. Buying indentures was a big thing in those days. Stables had a jockey, a lightweight jockey and an apprentice. I didn't have any say in the matter and Gerald turned the offer down.

I actually went to Harry Maw's for a couple of weeks and rode a few horses for him. I was seriously ill with the flu a couple of days before and was taken to digs, given hot black-currant and sent to bed. I felt sorry for the fellah that had to share a bed with me: Jack Berry. He was a jump jockey at Moore's and he looked after me through the flu. I remember Harry Moore giving me a big yellow pill the day I was riding for him. He said it would wake me up. I felt a million dollars and I went faster than his horse.

Then in 1962 Gerald started struggling. He was cutting down his horses and got rid of some of the lads. I was lucky. Being, I suppose, the one that was showing the most, I was kept. John and Dougy were given the choice of signing on for five years or going and they went. It was good for me in a sense because I learned so much more being in a small yard. I was made travelling head lad and was given a lot more respon-sibility, if only because of lack of staff. I was allowed to put bandages on a horse. It sounds nothing, but even some of the big stables don't allow staff to do that. I was also starting to learn about medication. I remember holding a horse called Saint Magic when he was fired and when he was gelded. He was gelded standing up and had a local anaesthetic. In a small yard you see all these things and learn a lot.

Pinkers Pond was owned by a Manchester Jew, Mr Bernstein. He was a bookmaker, I think. The horse had won at two and then became disappointing. He was getting a bit clever so they decided to put blinkers on him. Gerald found him a Catterick apprentices' race over seven furlongs, and I was told two days beforehand that if I could hold him, I could ride him in the race.

The morning before the race the blinkers were fitted and

Charlie Brown put me on him and told me to sit tight. Then he got the Long Tom, and gave the horse a few smacks round the hocks, where he couldn't see, just to tickle him up, to give him a fright – the normal thing to do when you put blinkers on first time. There were sparks coming out of his back feet because every time Charlie hit him he jumped forward. It was round by the dung hill and it smelled like a blacksmith's shop.

We went down through the park gates, along the bottom road towards Middleham and he worked five furlongs up the low moor. He actually walked past his namesake to get there: Pinkers Pond is a pond on the road past the bottom of the gallop. Anyway, I held him. I don't know how. Just through determination probably, because he was frightened and running with fear.

The most frightening thing about riding him was getting him to post. That day at Catterick I knew that Charlie Brown had tickled him up again, so the big problem was stopping him bolting before the race. I managed it somehow. I was not allowed the stick. Boys were never allowed the stick with Gerald. In all my early races I never had one. I had to ride all the way round.

There were seven runners, on firm ground. Pinkers Pond was 6-1. And he never saw another horse in the race. A pal of mine, Don Plant, who trained on and off for a bit, was second on a filly called Distance Enchanted. I beat him by six lengths.

I don't know about Gerald, but I was over the moon, sitting on the clouds. That first winner. It really got the adrenalin going. I thought, 'Lester Piggott, you've had it.' In the weighing room it was just an ordinary tiny race, but when I got back to Middleham we went out and had a celebration. I think I had quite a few friends in the yard because there were a few pennies on the horse.

There was no rush of winners after that but I did get a few more rides. They started to become a little more frequent, once a month or so. Then things actually started to dry up and I never came close to winning. I think Gerald was getting a little bit dried up, too, financially. He had decided to retire at the end of 1962. He hadn't told me, of course. In August he sent me down to his brother Sam's, for a few weeks, he said. Down

I went to Newmarket and I was there until Christmas. I read in the press that my trainer had retired, and I wondered what the hell was happening. Sam Armstrong was being a bit cagey – I think he wanted me to stay with him, but I was a free man.

Gerald had told him to get my indentures transferred. Sam wouldn't let me go home to Scotland until he got me signed up. Then he let me go for a couple of weeks' holiday.

I met my first wife, Carole, in Darlington. It was two or three months before I left to go to Newmarket. John, I think it was, had a car by then, a little old Austin Eight, and we used to go into Darlington to the café-bar. I wrote to Carole for a bit. Then I thought it was fading away.

On my way back from Scotland to Newmarket – with my mother – I went to Middleham to pick up all my old bits and pieces and I said, 'Let's call in at Darlington.' We got a bit of a shock. Carole hadn't told me and I don't think she was going to, either. She was far enough gone for me to think, 'Bloody hell, you've put weight on'. She was quite pleasant to me, which is possibly why I did what I did. If she'd been ranting and raving, it might have been different. She said well, it was her mistake as well as mine, so we decided to get married, near enough there and then. I think I just kept laughing. Mother was devastated.

I had to go back home again then to explain it to father. I locked myself in the loo. I was frightened of my dad, he was quite stern. He only ever hit me a couple of times. Once I think he got himself upset because he thought the gypsies had nicked me. I had gone to the fair and I was there with lads who didn't have to be home, but I was supposed to be in at ten. I got back at 11.30 so I shinned up the drainpipe and went to bed. And father woke me up and laid one into me. But he was very reasonable when I came out of the loo that day. He said, 'Well, son, you've made your bed, you're going to have to lie in it now, and we'll help you all we can.'

I went back down to Darlington and we got married within a week, in a registry office by special licence. The only wedding present I remember getting was from my parents: an electric blanket, which was marvellous.

Carole's parents were all right about it. Jack worked on the railways and did very little. He would go to work and sign on, then come back home and go to bed again. And then go back at night and sign off. But they worked hard on Sundays on the overtime, to make their wages up. He wasn't a well person. He was a quiet little fellah. He should have been a jockey, because he was lighter than me. He had the shakes from the war. He was on HMS Ajax and lucky for him missed it by half an hour the day it went down. He never really got over the war and he died of cancer quite young. The mother was a typical northern woman, very friendly, always got the kettle on, not very well educated and not very ambitious. They were friendly people, the sort that just lived from day to day.

After we were married I took Carole for a honeymoon at home, in my parents' house, for about four days. Then I dropped her off from the train at Darlington and went down to Newmarket. I didn't see her again until I went to Bogside to ride. She had already had her baby. It was the first time I'd seen it. I must be the only successful jockey that was virtually married, with a kid, before his second winner.

4

NEWMARKET

The bottom of the ladder, the very bottom rungs, but getting to Newmarket, and particularly to Sam Armstrong's, at least meant that he was onto them. What a long way up it must have looked in 1963.

It was the year of the Profumo scandal and the Great Train Robbery, of Cassius Clay being knocked down by Henry Cooper, of the Beatles knocking out the world at the London Palladium. Some of that might have registered with the wee Scotsman down from Middleham. But not half as much as Only For Life winning the Guineas, Relko the Derby and Piggott battling with Breasley for the jockeys' championship. He might have been at the bottom of the ladder but the institutionalising had begun.

No other sport, no other activity, envelops its participants the way the racing game can. There are not many of them at the coal-face. Trainers, jockeys, stable lads and officials would hardly muster three thousand head. But for those involved and for all the betting and media activity which follow in their wake, the whole of life is different, the calendar, even the map of the country, is redrawn. Without a racetrack to their name, Manchester, Birmingham and Bristol are missing; but Nottingham, Leicester and Bath remain. Spring is coming once you are through the Cheltenham Festival, midsummer is some-where between the Derby and Ascot week, autumn is here when racing has returned to Newmarket's Rowley Mile. Every day another meeting. Every dawn another chance. Every evening varied degrees of disappointment, occasionally sprinkled with the manna of success. That's the snakes and ladders of the Newmarket scene.

Young Billy had joined it.   U

Everybody was so smart in Newmarket. There weren't so many jeans and wellies. People wore jodhpurs. I was allowed some there. Everything was cleaner, too. And the strings were so much larger. At Middleham the biggest was Crump's, with about fifteen horses: tiny place Middleham, by comparison with Newmarket. You could notice the wealth difference.

The other great thing was that you went into people's homes, into digs. I stayed with the Smiths in a house just off Rowley Drive. I think they have gone to California now. They always used to have two Sam Armstrong boys and they treated you like one of the family. It was much better than being in a hostel.

Josh Gifford had lodged there before me and he was the big star, always being bragged about. There was a right bandit living there with me. He threw a brick through a shop window one night and nicked a doll for his sister's birthday. I remember running like hell that night. Funnily enough, when I was going to work the next morning the alarm bell was still ringing. Nobody had been out to investigate. We could have nicked the whole shop.

When I first went to Newmarket I kept in touch with Carole by writing and we had pre-assigned telephone times. It didn't seem odd at the time, although it would now. It was just the way it was. My father's words kept ringing in my head: you've made your bed, you've got to lie in it. That's what I was doing. I was quite happy. I was always trying to get a house, so that I could get Carole down. I was married and had no accommodation and I suppose Sam Armstrong was doing the best thing in a way. He sort of kept us apart. I had no money, anyway.

In the evenings I used to go to the bops in St Mary's Church Hall. It cost a shilling. I needed to sweat to keep my weight down and I'd always liked dancing. Then I had an idea: I put pyjamas on underneath my clothes and did some energetic jiving. Well, I had a good sweat all right, but suddenly I felt funny. I went outside and the cold air hit me. I'd only gone about twenty or thirty yards when I remember footsteps coming towards me. I grabbed the railings and then conked out. When I woke up there was nobody about. They must have thought I was drunk. There I was, still standing, hanging on to the railings. That was overdoing trying to get the weight off. Even so, when I was young I was always fainting if I jumped up suddenly. I don't know why. I went to the doctor's and he said there was nothing wrong. Nobody ever did find out what it was and I suppose I grew out of it.

It was my parents who decided that I should have a caravan so that my family could be together. We went to a site, Red Lodge, and met a couple called Geoff and Polly Miller. Geoff was a lovely guy. He'd just got married himself and of course he felt sorry for me so he organised the design of the caravan and arranged setting it up. The caravan was on hire purchase – mum and dad were paying most of it.

Red Lodge is on the way to Norwich, past the Limekilns and four or five miles out of Newmarket. I had to bike there and back twice a day. Twenty miles a day. So I became pretty fit. Sometimes, when the bike was out of order (and once when somebody nicked it) I had to walk, or run. In the end all the traipsing backwards and forwards became too much so Sam let me put the caravan in the little paddock at the yard. Then, during the winter, we moved it next to the bike shed. I was right on the spot then.

I don't remember much about how we coped in the caravan with a small child. Actually I don't think he ever cried much. He was a good kid. Carole seemed to fit in okay. She didn't work. She could typewrite and had been a secretary before we got married but only for six months or so. I used to go out with the lads, to the pub down the hill. We'd play shove ha'penny, and scrape up enough to buy half of beer.

In August I was out on strike for a couple of days with all the other lads. It was mostly Armstrong's boys, I think. We used to meet at Dino's, an Italian restaurant in Wellington Street. The owner kept giving us meals. I can't remember what the strike was about. Because I was now in the caravan in the yard I had a bit of extra pressure put on me to go back. Well, I did have a wife and a young kid and I was living in the caravan on his land, so I had to go back to work. The next day I went to Folkestone, got a ride and was second.

Later we moved out of the caravan, up to a house on Croft Road. Sam had decided to give me more wages then as I was twenty-one. He owned the house and took the rent out of my wages.

I was starting to get a ride once every two weeks and after a while they started to write about me – big stuff, my name in the newspapers! One press man, I don't recall who, asked what did I want to be known as: William, Billy, Bill, Will, Willie? And I said that Willie sounded nice and that's how I became Willie. At the time I was known as Scottie, especially up in Middleham. Some people still call me Scottie. I was known as Titch at school and mother always calls me Billy. But this press man christened me Willie and that stuck.

Although I was in Newmarket I was spending most of my time in the north. Coming back from the Scottish race meetings, the train would get to Peterborough but there was never a connection to Newmarket until the morning. From one o'clock till seven, when the first train left, I used to sleep in the waiting room flat out on a bench. When I woke up at about 6.30 there were always lots of people sitting around me, commuters going to work.

Sam Armstrong didn't give you the individual attention that Gerald did. Everything had been slower up north. Gerald was always teaching me how to ride, telling me what to do and how to behave. When I got to Newmarket I knew the rudiments of how to behave. But Sam thought the world of his boys and would go through fire for them. Even when they got into trouble he would always bail them out. We'd get a bollocking afterwards, of course, but he would always bail us out: 'My boys wouldn't do such a thing'. And he would take you in the car with him to the races and everything would be an education. He was always telling me things about what to do and how to do it: stand outside the weighing room, see

Mr So-and-so, fetch a cap and so on. And make yourself available all the time. Always be seen, he said. Stand outside the weighing room: unlike today, you could pick up spare rides because in those days they didn't have the jockeys down in the newspapers. And the papers only listed the possible runners, so you had to go to the betting shop to find out what was actually running.

I ended up the most successful apprentice they ever had until Ray Still broke my record of riding the most winners in a year as an apprentice. I came after lots and lots of jockeys and apprentices: Wally Swinburn had gone, so had Josh Gifford, but Michael Hayes was about. He had just finished his time. And Paul Tulk and Kipper Lynch had just left.

I always got to look after the nutty fillies at Sam's. He would come to look round every night. He was really military: you had to have your corn and your bedding made into a nice square, clean rubber out, tools turned upside down all cleaned up, and he'd check the tools just like your kit in the army. Then he would check your animal. One night he came to the third box and found this filly – looked after by a young apprentice, a new sixteen-year-old kid – looking at the kid, who was standing in the manger. Sam walked in and said, 'What are you doing in there, boy?' and he said, 'Talking to it, sir.' It's funny, she was virtually savage. She was going for this kid and he couldn't do anything about it. He was just standing in the manger trying to keep out of her way. So I ended up looking after her. She would hiss and spit at me, and one day she kicked me and lifted me off the ground, out of the box and into the yard. She was a little terror.

I got beaten on her by a short head and seemingly I did a bad job and should have won. She was odds-on and I was grounded. Sam said I wasn't getting any more rides for a month because I'd made a balls-up. People would ring up but he wouldn't let me ride. Anyway, time went on and I wasn't getting rides, and then Les Hall rang from the Leger meeting to say he desperately needed J. McKeown, another apprentice in Sam's yard, to ride a horse for him. He'd laid it out to win a particular race and it had finished fifth with Joe Mercer on and he was disappointed so he'd decided to run it again the next day. It only had seven stone six, so he wanted McKeown to ride.

McKeown was riding for Pat Taylor and wasn't available but Sam said that he had another boy that Hall might like to use: Carson. So I got the ride on the horse and it won at 9-1. I thought I was lucky, but Les Hall was apparently very much impressed and the following week he put me up on a filly called Last Report at Brighton and she won as well. And from that winner at Doncaster to the end of the season, which isn't very long, I rode ten winners. So Les Hall, in a way, was the man who set the ball rolling.

Life was definitely on the up. I was thinking about buying a little car and things like that. I bought a second-hand turquoise Mini, a great little car. I got it on hire purchase, in the hope that I would continue riding winners.

I was getting paid over a fiver more than the apprentices. Mind you, I was going on twenty-two. But I didn't get anything from the rides. Sam got half the fee and half the winnings and kept it, and you'd get it at the end of your apprenticeship. And you got nothing for riding a horse he trained himself. It was the normal arrangement. When you got a present for winning you had to take it home and give it to Sam. Though I might just have siphoned off a little bit first.

Our second child, Neil, was born at home, on 15 December, 1964. I helped to deliver him. The midwife had come to visit and it was decided that Carole should have it in the home – I don't know why. She started having contractions and I remember getting a bit of a panic on. I got her upstairs to bed but I didn't know what to do, and it was all starting to happen. I wouldn't look. I think that was the biggest panic in my life. I felt very helpless. I had the window wide open and every two or three minutes rushed to look for the midwife. I saw the baby's head appear. Carole was having a problem – the baby didn't come out because he had the cord round his throat. Then the midwife came, thank God, and within two minutes we had another son.

I got all the brown paper and took it downstairs to get rid of it. I'd just had a new bathroom built onto the two-up, two-down house. It hadn't been finished all that long. And it all fell through the paper, down the hole between the back door and the bathroom. I always remember that – splosh, it went, up the walls. I had to clean it all out.

I lost my claim in 1965, on Regal Bell, and rode my first treble, up in Scotland. My parents and uncle were there. Great day that was. The treble was for Ronnie Robson, quite a clever fellah who trained on a field next to Newcastle racecourse. I also won my biggest race, the Great St Wilfrid, on Monkey Palm.

The location, all the jockeys, overawed me a bit at first – you always used to get a bollocking off the older jockeys. Nowadays it's the kids who tell us what to do. But then you were half-expected to get out of the way of a top jockey. Scobie and Lester were the riding kings at that time. Scobie was my idol: he was the one guy you were always worried about coming past and getting you on the winning post. And of course there was Lester. At that time I was sort of getting horses ready for him. I'd ride them at 20-1, then he'd get on and all of a sudden it'd be 6-4 on and he'd win.

The dirty work was always done in wording that I understood. 'This horse is not quite a hundred per cent, he will be better for the race, we have got him well entered.' That meant they didn't want the bloody thing today. But with Sam you never, ever stopped a horse that was going to win. If a horse was good enough to win you'd be told to win on it – though he did sometimes say he'd rather it won by a short head. But for other trainers you got on a few no-goers. That happened in those days. I don't recall ever facing the possibility of trouble; when you were told not to win on them, they were horses that weren't going to win anyway or at least weren't expected to.

I remember riding a horse called Parcel Post. I had won on it in August 1964 at Chepstow. I took my hands off and the stewards had me and gave me a rollocking because although I'd looked round both ways and hadn't seen anything, Flapper

Yates came and I only beat him a head. I should have won by a long way. Later in the season we went to Doncaster and I was telling all my friends that this horse would win. I think Willie Snaith rode one for Sam Armstrong, a grey filly which was favourite, and I said, I'll beat that. Old Arthur Thomas, who trained Parcel Post, thought it would win as well. It beat Armstrong's at 50-1. After the race Arthur Thomas must have been to the bookmakers and collected his money because I remember him peeling off tenners. He gave me fifty quid. I thought it was an absolute fortune.

1965 was a good year. I was getting talked about as a good lightweight jockey. At that stage I had no silly ambitions about being champion. I just wanted to be a good lightweight with a good stable, which was quite a good living. Of course I wanted to win, and to keep improving, and the more success I got the more I wanted.

Sam Armstrong told me to find somebody of similar stature to myself, watch him and copy him. He said the best fellah for me to watch would be Doug Smith. Watch him, he said, and try to do what he does. I suppose I did try, but I didn't come out like Doug Smith.

After I'd bought the car, the next big dream was owning a house and that came along soon afterwards. I bought 5 Churchhill Avenue for £3,695. I still own it and it's worth a hundred grand now. Family life was fine then. No real problems. I had a very happy time. I wasn't expecting anything: I had no money, no worries and a lot of friends all in the same boat. The dream was always to better oneself. When I first got the Mini I was struggling so I used to charge all the kids two bob to go across to Cambridge to roller-skate. Then I had another idea. If I got the missus to cook something when I got back, I could charge them two and sixpence for supper. I used to bring them all back and feed them sausages, beans, eggs and toast. We had a lodger as well, one of the kids from Armstrong's, so that all helped.

Family holidays were going back to Darlington or up to Scotland. I always had to go to Scotland for the New Year, that was a big thing for me. We had to get the house all cleaned up. Everything had to be spick and span for the New Year coming in. We all stayed at home and had a little drink and put clean clothes on just before midnight. Then we'd switch on the TV and watch Andy Stewart bring in the New Year and I'd have a hug and a kiss and a drink. Then we'd either go out or wait for the first-footer to knock on the door. If he was tall, dark and handsome, you would be lucky. He'd have a bit of coal in one pocket to put on the fire to keep you warm, and a bottle in the other. You always have to have a bottle in your pocket and to drink out of everybody else's. I used to go first-footing with my father. You'd walk down the street and into people's houses. You never knew who they were but you'd always be invited in for a drink. They were great, friendly times.

When I came out of apprenticeship with Sam in 1965 I was given a nest-egg of £1,100 from the rides. I don't think I had a bank account then. I paid off my debts with it. In 1966 Sam offered me a little retainer, £500, to be his lightweight jockey. He sort of kept me under his wing, though in other words I was still working for him in the mornings.

When I had a few winners I used to pay the apprentices a couple of bob to muck my horse out and tack it up so that I could have an extra ten minutes in bed. I've never been good at getting up in the mornings and was always in trouble for being late. When we had the caravan in the paddock, the second head man used to shake it and bang on the window to get me up. One morning Sam hit me right across the face with the Long Tom because I was late. I didn't like that at all but back in the early sixties there wasn't so much liberation. I was a servant. I'd been brought up as a servant and I didn't think there was anything wrong in that. I knew my place. I didn't know any different.

Sam was marvellous. When he made out his list of what you were riding in the morning he typed everything out and made comments in red beside the names: 'Still hasn't had hair cut', or 'Rides too short, drop your length', all different things about what you did. About me, he'd put comments about my

being late: 'Try to be on time'. And there were always comments about the horses – 'tack looked dirty' – and so on. We
used to run round and shout, 'So-and-so's getting a bollocking'
because of something on the list. It was incredible how he was
always putting people straight, keeping things going.

Sam was a big influence on me and so was Gerald – he was
perhaps the biggest influence of all. In fact, the Armstrong
family *are* me: they are my success. And I made both men very
proud of me.

5
LORD DERBY'S JOCKEY

As he looks back now it's hard to see Carson as a lackey. He sits at the smartest tables, he's got a pretty good one of his own. On any day he might talk on equal terms with the Queen, Lord Weinstock or Sheikh Hamdan al Maktoum. The bow-legged passport has worked again. It always has. The jockey won't pay for the horse, the owner can't ride it. They are united in a relationship whose stability is totally balanced on success. If either party is unable to match the other's ambition, the pairing is doomed. Every horse, every ride, renews the ambition. If they are into a run of success, the bonding tightens like linking threads of a rope. If they are on a losing streak, the unravelling is just the same.

But it remains a relationship and in a small and jealous pond there is always the thought of fresh partners. There is an element of dating the new girl in the class, of seeking and being sought. Actors have it, soccer players too, but maybe none so promiscuous, so instantly startable as the booking of the jockey. After all, it is the horse which does the running: put a leg either side, avoid any arguments and romance is under way. Have you tried Carson, that little Scots kid at Armstrong's? By 1966 it was an engagement an increasing number liked to make.

For the young hustler every ride is a bonus but the real account is that of self-belief. As an apprentice, part of the induction process is to lionize the top jockeys of the day, the mystical masters of the craft whose very boots the boys are not fit to shine. Not only do they have much more skill and experience, they also ride the best horses. The pilot on the make can apply himself to the skill. The other two elements take time. And, most of all, they require outside support.

Which, in racing's strangely feudal way, is where the Lords and the Masters come in.   ∪

I got a message: go and see the Guv'nor. When you went up to Sam's office it was usually for a bollocking. But we didn't go into the office. He took me into the hallway where he kept the daybook. The daybook showed when you were going away racing. While you were waiting to see him you always peered in it to see what he had written.

He started off by saying that Doug Smith had decided to retire and that Lord Derby would like to know if I would be interested in taking the job for him. My heart had been down in my boots because I'd been expecting problems. It ended up in my mouth. Lord Derby's jockey? Me? Sam went ranting on about a few little things and then said that I had a week to think about it. He told me to go home, talk to Carole and think about it. And I said, 'Sir, I don't have to think about it. I'll start now, okay?' There wasn't any 'How much?' or anything like that. And he said, 'Well, boy, very wise, very wise, wise decision, wise decision, I shall tell him.'

So I had to go round to meet Bernard van Cutsem. Bernard van Cutsem: the most terrifying trainer there was. He had employed Eph Smith, who died. I actually saw Eph the morning before it happened. I spoke to him. There were times when he seemed to be a bit vague. It was a shame he committed suicide. He was on too many pills, that was the problem. He was drinking, but he had too many pills as well. He could never go to the races without being sick.

I turned up at Bernard's. I took the car round the corner, walked up to the office door and knocked. He seemed quite nice. Very upright and to the point. I had to go to see Lord Derby at Newmarket – Stanley House. That was a great big grand house. Only small compared to some, perhaps, but to me it was enormous. And he said I would get a house to go with the job. I was living in Churchill Avenue in a small, three-bedroomed semi-detached. And I got Falmouth Cottage. It was a mansion! It was three storeys and had five bedrooms. Carole and I used to peer through the hedge and look at it, saying, cor, it's gorgeous.

Lord Derby was aristocracy and one of the top men of the Jockey Club, the hierarchy. All the big owners were Lords in those days: Rosebery, Derby. In a way Lord Derby was thought of as Sheikh Hamdan is today. When I went in it was all very formal. It was very much 'Sir', 'My Lord'. I had put my best clobber on: drainpipe trousers, narrow-lapel jacket and a little thin black tie. When I told Carole we had a big celebration. Now we had the chance of going somewhere.

I started riding out there in February or March. I polished my boots up and got new jodhpurs for that. At the time I didn't think I was up to the top jockeys' standard but I was starting to have a bit more confidence in myself. I thought I could do it but I didn't think I would be a Piggott or a Breasley. The great thing was that now I was going to have horses of my own. I wasn't going to be getting them ready for somebody else. They were going to be mine and whatever I did with them I was going to be riding them next time. That was the thing that hit me.

At first I was given only eight horses. Doug Smith hadn't retired then – he was going to go on for one more year. I was being pushed in gradually. So Doug rode all the best ones and I was told that my eight were mine to ride all the time. Russ Maddock was riding the non-Lord Derby horses.

I had more trouble with the lads than I had with Bernard. They didn't fancy me at all. I didn't have rows with them but we used to see them all rabbiting. Not so much in the beginning, but it was there: I could hear rumours that this young lightweight was not up to it. Doug was very good to me. I don't know for sure, but I believe it was Doug who put my name forward. I had thirty-five winners that season, so I didn't lose ground on the previous year.

I was always trying to be lighter. I had a sauna put in at Falmouth Cottage and I was in it every day. I was trying to be two pounds lighter than my body wanted me to be. The same two pounds went on and came off every day. I ate reasonably normally but if I had a light ride I didn't eat as much. Nowadays I accept a normal riding weight, which for me some days is seven stone ten, while others it might be seven-nine or seven-eleven. That's normal and I don't interfere with it. When I started riding for Lord Derby I was trying to do seven-seven.

I don't think it was ever in doubt that I would be confirmed as Lord Derby's jockey that winter. I was always under the impression that I was definitely taking over the following year and of course that was why I was there, watching the two-year-olds, so that when I did take over I would be in control of things. Bernard van Cutsem was always the sort of person who mapped out races for his horses a year in advance. His planning was systematic.

When Lord Derby was staying at Newmarket it was not unknown for him to pop in for a coffee, or I would go and see him when he wanted to know something. I only went to the stud once. It was much later, when the bust-up with Carole came. It was between Christmas and New Year – I suppose it was in the press. I was summoned to Knowsley to see him. I didn't know whether I was going to get a rollocking or what. I drove all the way up from Newmarket. I had a silver Mercedes 232E. I used to call her Mildred. When I arrived I parked Mildred outside, along from the front door. I rang the bell and was taken in by a butler. It was a grand house. I was taken to the drawing-room where I was met by Lord Derby.

We had tea and then I felt like a cigarette – I was smoking in those days. I excused myself and popped out to the car. But it wasn't there. Apparently it had been taken to the garage for the night. So I mentioned a cigarette and suddenly a packet was produced in a gold box with the Derby emblem on them: specially made for Lord Derby.

After that I was shown to a room. What temperature would you like the bath, sir? That was a poser. What temperature? Hot! My bag had been taken out of the car. I had a scruffy old toilet bag, grease and all sorts in it, everything just chucked in. All this had been laid out on a lovely white cloth on the dressing table. My clothes had been taken out of the suitcase and put in drawers. The butler asked me what I would like in the morning. That was an education, that was.

When the car turned up the next day it was spotless. It had been really scruffy because there was snow on the roads, salt and all sorts. Yet the car was spotless. They must have spent all night cleaning it.

At dinner that night the subject was my situation. There was just Lord and Lady Derby and they wanted to be informed of what I was up to. They weren't difficult with me, they just wanted to know first hand what was happening with my marriage. And they accepted it. They didn't say they disapproved, but how could they? I reckon Lady Derby was naughty anyway. She was a great girl. She would always make me feel at ease. He could be a bit stuffy but she was always friendly: she came down to stable lads' talk, which was reassuring.

She went racing a lot but she never came into the paddock before a race so you didn't know she was there. She would always come to you afterwards to find out what had gone on. After Bernard died in 1975 the horses went to John Winter, a lovely little gentleman. I was riding a chestnut horse, no great star, just a handicapper who was thought to be a bit high in the handicap. Lord Derby, a member of the Jockey Club – always running horses on their merits. . . Well, we thought, the horse should have a run up at Newmarket. And I came past the bushes swinging off him. I was in a bit of a dilemma: should I pull or push? I thought, to hell with this, and I gave him a push and got beat a head. So the plan was neither here nor there. Lady Derby came, just as I was getting the saddle off, put her head between mine and John Winter's, and said: 'Now then, Carson, what the fucking hell were you up to?' I can remember John Winter being shocked – he didn't expect it from her. She was a little angry, but she was making fun of it all.

6
ACCIDENT

It's not only fractured bones which become stronger as they heal. The country would be a far more purposeful place if everybody had to go through a hospital recovery from a broken limb. The Worshipful Company of Sadists could have the time of its life smashing arms and legs to cause it.

Incentive is the best medicine. It's quite astonishing how quickly you can recover if a good ride is in the offing. The special plaster cast, the adapted technique, the heightened awareness, the absolute denial of pain. But that is in the short term when only one bit of you is missing. With the bigger smash-ups it is rather different. Suddenly there is a doubt whether you will ever mend. Not just in your mind but in others'. 'You'll be up and about soon,' they suggest comfortingly, as they survey the wreckage with hungry eyes. You know what they are going to say as soon as they can get their hands on the phone. 'I have just seen him,' they hiss, looking back down the corridor for eavesdroppers. 'He looks terrible, wires and drips all over the place. I can't see how he will ever ride again.'

Today there is hardly a mark on him. Willie Carson may be a veteran amongst the 'knights of the pigskin', but he must be one of the healthiest fifty-year-olds in the kingdom. The stamina built from paper rounds, dog-fox runs and thirty years pumping in the saddle has never been sapped by 'wasting' for too long. The crashes of a jockey's life have caused their grief and, as we will later see, some agonizing moments of uncertainty. But the worst came from a car, not a horse. And if the little Scotsman was a hard case before, he was set to be even tougher after.

For this wasn't minor. This could be curtains. This could mean 'finish' when the big things hadn't even begun.   ∪

8 November 1966. It was exactly a week after racing had finished. I had just taken delivery of a new Jag. I'd had it a week. After the Mini I'd had a Renault, then a Ford Corsair – the engine fell out of that on the A1 on the way to Beverley – and now I had this Jag. It was one of those two-door jobs, really nice. It was second hand, but it was a 3.8 automatic, a big, powerful car.

We had had the jockeys' dinner the night before. I had stayed the night in London and got home about midday. It was a bit foggy and we wanted to get off to Darlington. We should never have gone. I said we'd go as far as Cambridge, because I wanted to go to the garage – there was something wrong with the radio, I think. We went to the garage and got it seen to. And we had to make a decision: do we go home or don't we? We were all packed up so we thought, let's go. It was foggy then and it was foggy all the flaming way. And we had the accident.

We were on a dual carriageway at Aberford, just before Wetherby, before the Tadcaster turning where you go off for York. There's a garage there. Just half a mile back to the south, by Aberford, it was foggy and suddenly there was this wagon, coming down the other side and doing a U-turn to go north. Doing a U-turn on the dual carriageway. And I think he had a trailer on the back, which I hit. The fellah in the wagon was fined £15. I was fined a fiver because my licence had run out. This guy nearly kills a family and he gets fined £15. I get fined a fiver because I've forgotten to renew my licence.

Carole thinks I fell asleep and I can't remember, everything just went blank. But I couldn't have been asleep because I swerved. The fog was quite thick and I was going too fast. I was doing about forty mph when I should only have been doing about five mph. By this time I should think I was getting fatigued. All I remember is driving up the road and just seeing my lights shine up on to that bloody thing in front of me. I didn't know what it was. I just remember the lights, and swerving.

Three of us broke femurs. I suppose it was with all the weight going on to one leg. Carole was in the passenger seat and young Neil must have been standing somewhere in between. Tony was lying asleep on the back seat. There were no seat belts. I went underneath the wagon. My head was sticking through the windscreen and the windscreen was way back. My toe was nearly in my mouth. The wheel was in the radio.

It was dark. Ten past six at night it happened. For some reason I didn't have shoes on. They must have been hurting and I'd taken them off. I was going in and out of consciousness. I heard Carole screaming. I think somebody came along and took the kids out. They were screaming, too. I had chewing gum in my mouth and I thought it was my gum. The teeth were all smashed in the chewing gum and there was blood everywhere. The pain was killing me.

Somebody came along and took my tie off and tied my leg to the steering wheel to hold it up. The police arrived, then the fire brigade. The fire brigade couldn't get at me. They had to use crowbars to open the door. And Carole was still in the car. It was the ambulance man who came in. 'George, have a look at the driver, he looks a goner,' I heard. I thought, 'Oh. He looks a goner, that's what he said, he looks a goner.' I said, 'I ain't gone yet.'

They kept coming and going. They finally got the car door open but they couldn't get me out. I screamed. My leg must have been still tied to the steering wheel. I suppose it was quite funny, trying to pull me out of the car with my leg still tied up. I had a lovely brand new blue suit on and a pocketful of readies, all my readies from the year: we'd been saving up to go on holiday.

It was two and a half hours before we got to hospital. We all went together in the same ambulance. I woke up once but I don't remember much about it. But I do remember being wheeled in. They didn't give me any painkillers, because the surgeon on duty that that night was against painkillers. It was quite a traumatic time. I remember waking up in hospital. A nurse was counting my money. I remember her saying that she and her ma could go back home with that money and have a good holiday, or something like that.

Then I was lying in a corridor, on a low stretcher, in agony. Lying in the corridor because they wouldn't operate until a certain amount of time had passed: I had been eating and they were afraid I would be sick. Then, after the operation, who did I wake up to? Just a blur: a white collar, 'Shall we pray'. Shall we pray! Phew, gone again. I don't remember seeing him any more. The next thing I saw were the nurses. Drips in my arm. I was in agony. I had twenty-seven stitches in my face and a broken jaw.

Carole, who was pregnant with Ross at the time, had smashed her leg up. Virtually all she did, apart from a cut, was thump herself on the crutch and smash her leg. They wouldn't let her get up. She was still in hospital with her broken leg in a splint when Ross was born, seven months later. Neil had a broken leg, too, but he was a kid and got over it very quickly. Anthony had a cut on his head, a bit of concussion. He was discharged the next day.

We'd been taken to St James's Hospital, Leeds – Jimmy Saville's place. I heard about him while I was in there. He was working there as a porter, wheeling people about. But I never bumped into him. When we had been sorted out we were sent up to Ilkley, the old TB hospital up on the moor, to recuperate. It was the overspill for St James's for people like us. Two died while I was there. It was funny: the women were on one side and the men on the other and they used to wheel us together. Little Neil was with his mother. I was stuck there in traction for over three months.

It was a very traumatic time, lying in pain in hospital, feeling as though I was going to cry. Something was telling me that I would never ride again. Before, I'd had nothing to lose but now I had, and I didn't want to lose it. They were soul searching times, for a few days, weeks even. I was feeling low. I was in shock. The doctors said there would be no permanent damage, but of course the riding was a worry. I just had to sit there and wait it out.

I was looked after very well. Although I wasn't exactly a personality, people had heard of me, just. There were two nurses, a male nurse and his wife, who were very good to me. I send them a card every year.

Time went by. I had been to the doctors at Newmarket General Hospital and they had taken X-rays. I was expecting them to say that I was all right and could go ahead, but they told me to wait another month. So I wasn't going to make it to the start of the Flat. Then I was down in Barry Hills's cottage, next to the yard, and we watched Maddock win on a horse of Lord Derby's called Laureate. That was at Liverpool, the Union Jack Stakes, a big race in those days, a Guineas trial. And Barry said I got up and threw my crutches away.

I wasn't even working then. But the next day I got on Mick Ryan's pony – Mick worked as travelling head lad at Bernard's. I got on the pony and rode round. And nothing broke. I remember going for a canter on this pony: it was do or die. And the leg didn't break. I had no feeling from it, no pain. So I did my own physio, didn't discuss it with a doctor. I had a calliper splint on, a metal thing with a ring. It went through a hole in your shoe and kept your leg straight. When you walk you click it straight and you walk on your hip, not your leg. I took the calliper off. It was a calculated risk, but it worked out.

I didn't feel a hundred per cent fit, though. I think it was a week later that I put the calliper back on and went to the hospital. When the doctor said I could take it off now I smiled. He asked me why I was smiling so I told him what I'd done. He said I seemed to have got over the worst so I could carry on. I was fit and riding again by the end of April.

On my first day back, at Thirsk, I rode a filly that Doug Smith trained for Lord Derby and she was a right little so-and-so. Cantering down to the start she stuck her toes in and I went straight over her head, right in front of the stands. I landed on my leg. I got up – and that gave me all the confidence in the world because I knew then that it would be all right. The leg was okay and I rode a winner, for Harry Blackshaw, in the last race. The horse was owned by a chauffeur and was called The Pack Horse and it won at 6-1. Lord Derby's horse Laureate ran on the same card in the Thirsk Classic Trial but I wasn't allowed to ride him. Russ Maddock did and he came third.

Laureate in the Derby was my first Classic ride. I'd won the Dee Stakes at Chester on him. He'd won three races and would definitely stay. He was a live outsider. He had a bit of temperament, though. He was a bit of a hard puller and I remember coming round Tattenham Corner, with Sandy Barclay just in front of me, and I was going just as well as him. He was riding Connaught. I had high hopes then but we got a furlong down the straight and bang, bang, Laureate blew up, his heart went or whatever. He was gone, finished virtually last. I was devastated. It was one of the big disappointments of my life.

Dear me, the Derby. I was as nervous as a kitten. I think Bernard was, too. You could always tell with Bernard: he would light a cigarette, take two puffs, and out it would go. Then another one would come out, light up, another two puffs, and down that would go. That was when he had money on. He never told me but I could tell. He'd stand there looking down at a packet of cigarettes all stamped on.

Bernard van Cutsem was a person who instilled confidence in me. He had all the jockeys terrified of him. When I first went there I was terrified of him as well. But after a while he would invite me over to dinner at Northmore and I'd go racing with him. And when I made a mistake I would always tell him. I never tried to kid him or bluff my way through. If I thought I should have ridden a horse differently I always told him. After a while he would ring me up and tell me not to worry, everybody makes mistakes. So we turned full circle really. In a way he treated me as more than just a jockey. He used to tell me how to invest my money. He was far ahead of his time, too. He used to talk about centralised racing and horses being trained on the American system in this country – which is all just starting to come through now.

It was Bernard who advised me to get a mare. I'd ridden a filly called Pussy Pelmet and although she wasn't very good herself I knew there were one or two coming on from that family. So when she came up for sale I bought her, from Humphrey Cottrill. I boarded her in the shed at Falmouth Cottage, bedded on Bernard van Cutsem's straw. I got Jock Brown, Clive Brittain's head lad, to come and look after her. She's bred some winners since.

I never had an accountant. I've always left managing the money to the wife. When I first went to work for Lord Derby I had a bit of money and I had a bank account with Lloyds. When I moved into Falmouth Cottage Stan Clayton, who was moving out, wanted paying for the doorknobs, the lightbulbs and so on. I think he robbed me but I didn't want a row so I paid for them. I wrote him a cheque for £200 and it bounced: the only cheque I've ever written that bounced.

When I heard about it I got hold of Barry Hills, because I knew he played golf with the Midland Bank manager, Nobby Clarke. Barry told me to go to the Coach and Horses for a drink at lunch-time and he'd introduce me. When I told Nobby Clarke about my problem he said that he'd have my account transferred to the Midland and I could have an overdraft of two hundred quid. I've stuck with the Midland ever since. I've lived away from Newmarket since 1977 but my bank account is still there.

I didn't get the bank manager to invest my money for me, though. I did that myself. I invested it in houses in Newmarket. I thought it would be a good idea to rent them out to American servicemen. They were always crying out for accommodation and they would always give you the top rent. They were all new houses, because there was a big building boom on. I bought one every now and again and ended up with eight. They cost about £8,000 each. All I had to do was put in carpets, curtains and a cooker. Bernard van Cutsem used to call me a little Rachman.

It was 1968 and I was still thought of as a good lightweight. I was still trying to keep my weight down, worrying about doing seven stone seven. I didn't mind. I was doing well, better than most. At the end of that year Russ Maddock lost the job as Bernard van Cutsem's jockey. Russ was quite a decent jockey but he did a couple of things wrong. One morning he rode Park Top. I wasn't in the gallop – Bernard was very fair, he never asked me to do dirty work on horses I wasn't going to ride. It seemed that Maddock hadn't done enough work with Park Top and Bernard was raging. He said, 'I've a good mind to send you down and work it again.' Maddock was ranting and raving and Bernard didn't know what to do. He was absolutely livid. That was the start of the end.

The other thing Russ did that didn't help his cause was riding his finish one circuit too soon in a race at Chester over two miles two furlongs. I was actually in that race. We had gone just over a mile and a quarter and we were coming to the three-furlong marker when all of a sudden Russ made a quick move. I was on the inside and I looked at the other jockeys to see what their reaction was. I could see that everybody else was thinking the same as me: we had to go round again. When he got to the furlong marker Russ grabbed hold of his horse, tap, tap, and won by a cosy three lengths. When he got round the corner and started to ease up and go a little bit wide, the whole field went whizzing by him. I felt really sorry for him. He had to file back into the field and try to ride the horse again. Of course, the horse ran shockingly and I don't think Bernard was best pleased. The relationship ended at the finish of that season. I sort of took over the whole stable then. I wasn't retained, I was still Lord Derby's jockey, but I started riding most of van Cutsem's horses on a more regular basis.

Bernard was quite a card. He had a big Mercedes with his own number plate and always had a chauffeur. I used to sit in the back and everybody thought I was the personality. He always sat in the front with his chauffeur. He used to wear a seat belt before they were compulsory. He had his stock of cigarettes, his own special brand, in the cubby hole. He was the last of the gentleman trainers, a proper aristocrat.

When I had dinner with him he seemed to take pleasure in getting me pissed. I used to get a bit worried about it. I was trying to sip and he'd say, 'Come on, boy, does you good.' He was of the Noel Coward ilk when he walked – big and tall. He used to go to London and he'd be in the casino all night long, get forty winks in the car on the way back and go on to the yard and be there before anybody else. Then he'd have another forty winks in the car going to the races and be ready to play cards all night long again. They tell me he was a proper gambler. He would lose everything. And it wouldn't worry him. He'd just keep on going and get it all back again. His expression never changed. I went down with him a few times but he always told me, 'Don't bother with gambling, you never win.'

The women loved him. He was always getting himself involved. He didn't marry but there was a woman who took his name. She was around most of the time that I was there. Sandie Shaw was before her. Bernard had a big row with Humphrey Cottrill, one of his mates, over Sandie Shaw.

Bernard was part of my education, really. He taught me how to speak and he taught me to tell the truth. I think the only time I got into trouble with him was for being late.

7

NEW HORIZONS

You can see them from the air. Anywhere in the world. Those tell-tale ovals that can mean only one thing. Down there they have racehorses, and anyone who can ride them has a chance of a job.

From that principle you get the winter exodus. British-based jockeys flying off like swallows in search of the winter sun. Turn up after Christmas in Kuala Lumpur, Sha Tin, Calcutta, especially in the new-found operation in Dubai, and you will find names normally seen on number boards at Newbury, Newcastle and the like. It's their luck that Britain and especially Newmarket has been the fountainhead of the game. On summer trips the big players of the orient and afar still tend to visit Ascot and Epsom to see how the old firm does it. An introduction then can mean that the frost never comes again.

In many ways it is the most divisive cut of all. For stable lads, apprentices and jockeys on the struggle, flat racing's close season during the winter months means long, cold, dark mornings of drudgery. Your waterproofs begin to leak. The yearling you have been given for second lot is a head case. The Guv'nor has pushed off on holiday like that jammy little Carson git. There are no runners from the yard to help the punters. The wife's moaning about fixing the attic. There's no justice in the world.

Be that as it may, it happens. And if it happens to you the trick, as you will read, is to keep your eyes open – and your hands up.   U

As my reputation grew, doors began to open throughout the racing world. There was America, South Africa and India. From there I was lucky to make it home.

I went to Florida to work for Tommy Kelly. I enjoyed it to begin with but it was a bit boring towards the end. There I was – a successful jockey – virtually being a work lad: cleaning tack every morning and riding out. I had done all that before. The first six weeks were great but then there was nothing happening, no rides. What kept me there was Tommy Kelly. He was a very nice person. He rented a house for the whole winter, when they all drove down from New York to Miami. He had a big family, Irish. He looked after his horses magnificently. He was always very concerned about their feet. I learnt a lot from him. The Americans can teach us a good deal because they have many more problems than we do.

In fact, the trip did me a lot of good. My riding improved, mainly regarding pace. I learnt how to ride the clock and I rode some nice horses. The top jockey at the time was Jorge Velasquez. I told myself it was no good trying to be English – they weren't interested in that. You had to try to be a bit more like their jockeys. Maybe I didn't adapt quickly enough because I only got one ride even though Jane Goldstein fought for me tooth and nail, got stories in all the papers about me. The horse I rode was called Check Board and it finished last. It was shipped next day to Bowie, the equivalent of our Catterick. It was useless. I suppose the ride was there just to keep me happy.

During the day we would go sight-seeing, or down on the beaches, have picnics. It was a great life. I took a few days off and went to Orlando to see Disney World. It was absolutely amazing. You'd think it was just for kids, but it's not. The grown-ups enjoy it more than the kids do.

Everybody was really interested in American football and I caught the fever, too. When I was in Miami the Dolphins were doing well. They were in the Superbowl, the big thing of the year, and I was there while it was happening. I went to one of their matches and it was marvellous. It's a totally different atmosphere from English football. You wouldn't be worried about taking the kids. Everybody sits down and you're there to be entertained.

I'd been riding for Colin Crossley and we did a few things together. I got really into hi-li. Nearly every night I went to watch this game, where they throw a ball against a wall at the end of a hundred-metre court. Betting on that was my big kick.

To begin with I used to go racing a lot in the afternoons, then I got bored with that. I'd made a few bucks on a little grey horse called Here Comes Trouble. He had had leg trouble and always ran in claiming races under what he was worth. I got Colin into it, and he made a few bucks on him, too. When he came home he bought a grey horse and named it Here Comes Trouble but I'm afraid the English version wasn't quite like the American.

I met Cassius Clay one day. He was training in Miami. You paid a dollar to get into the gym on Fifth Street Avenue. We were in there one day and Colin said he didn't see too many English people around so he muscled in and said, 'We are from the *Daily Express*.' He got us an introduction to Angelo Dundee. He could see that Cassius Clay was being interviewed by Italian TV, so he grabbed hold of me and threw me up against Cassius. He didn't know what was coming. As I bumped into him, Cassius put his hands up and said, 'Don't hit me, don't hit me please.' There I was, this tiny little fellah, and he was going: 'Don't hit me'.

I'd never seen boxers sparring before and it happened to be the day that all the press were there. Cassius Clay was a show-man – he put on a show as if it was theatre. Marvellous. And of course he had all the actions and expressions that make you chuckle.

I went out to South Africa a few times as well. They were the first to have an international jockeys' meeting and they had the best horses for us to ride, with a lot of money at stake. We went to Pietermaritzberg, then to Durban, then to Cape Town and Johannesburg. The places were all very different. We had some fantastic trips, great fun. Went up to the Valley of the Seven Hills, near Durban, with the Zulu tribe.

There wasn't much trouble with apartheid at that stage. When I went there the blacks were under strict control and as far as I could see there were no arguments and nobody was complaining.

In the members' ring, there were all whites. And then it turned to all black. We rode past a sea of faces which would just change colour, from colourful, because all the whites wore different clothes, to black, because all the blacks dressed quite alike.

The whole family went to India. We were there for three months, from December to February. Wally Swinburn was the top man then. Young Walter went to school with Tony.

Going to Calcutta would have been exciting for anybody. I think everyone should see Calcutta: it changes one's outlook on life, broadens one's horizons. Seeing the poverty is an experience. It wasn't as bad when I went there as it used to be, but there was still tremendous hardship. You could bribe the policemen if you drove down a one-way street the wrong way. Once when I got caught I gave him a couple of rupees and that was the end of it.

One misty morning, before the sun came up, I was talking to Dinky Fownes, the man I was riding for. There were two kids there, aged seven and four, with big smiles on their faces. I thought it was a bit early for kids that age to be up. They were orphans, didn't know what parents were. They lived in a big place called Victoria Memorial and went around begging. They were happy. A seven-year-old looking after a four-year-old. Incredible.

We lived on the ground floor of a little hotel. We had quite a big room with a fan and a bathroom, very little carpet. It was dark, but adequate. We had beds for the kids. Once I saw a tail about a foot long going underneath the bed. I thought, Jesus, the rats must be some size, but it wasn't a rat. They have something else bigger than that. Bloody great thing it was. It went whoosh, down the hall and got out that way. There was a mesh to stop these creatures getting in but it had been moved.

Outside in the city there were wild monkeys. One of them scratched Neil across the face and drew blood. We were very concerned about tetanus and the doctor had to be called in.

The racecourse was right in the centre of Calcutta, surrounded by poverty. India was a big education for me. I was twenty-eight but still a boy at heart, learning all about life.

We had two servants. That was a big thrill. There was a little woman who looked after the kids and I had a bearer, a thin old fellah called Sam. He was dressed all in white. He did anything I wanted him to do. Called me Sahib. Having a slave took a bit of getting used to. I'd send him on little errands, give him two rupees and tell him to get such and such. Of course, he always came back with the wrong thing. He only worked when I was out there. When I came home he didn't work for nine months. He wrote to me, saying, 'If you come back, Sahib, I work for you.'

They raced once a week, on Saturdays. During the rest of the week I'd get up very early and ride about eight horses. It was quite a nice track. It still is nice, hasn't changed at all. For the rest of the day I'd sleep or play snooker or golf. There were a lot of country club-type places but I never became that keen on golf or tennis. If I had my time again I would persevere at doing something but I just mucked around, doing a bit of everything. I can remember playing squash with the Indian champion, though I wasn't much good at it. It was a great social place. We were always going to parties. I didn't get stomach upsets or anything. I've always been quite lucky. And I do like experimenting with food, changing my diet and tasting new things.

Then there was the riot. We'd just finished the second race and Brian Taylor had been beaten a head by a 33-1 shot from the same stable. Matt Goldstein, the trainer, did used to pull a few strokes, but I don't think this was one of them. When we went out into the paddock for the third race I heard a pinging noise. People were throwing stones at the metal number board. I didn't take much notice and everybody just carried on as usual. We got on our horses and were about to take them on to the track when someone stopped us and told us to turn back. I looked down the track and we could see fires starting up. People were pulling the rails off and setting them on fire. Charming.

So we took the horses back. Then things started to get seriously out of hand. The police charged down the course waving batons then, all of a sudden, turned round and ran for

ABOVE: I wasn't interested in school. I could tell I wasn't going to be Prime Minister. That's me right at the front on the right

BELOW: I knocked around, did all the normal things that other boys did . . . playing football, nicking apples. Great fun

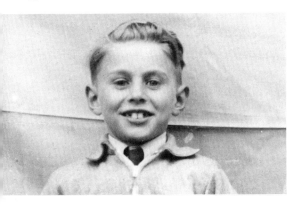

RIGHT: I loved playing round at Grandfather's. That's him on the right. He had everything: greyhounds, pigeons, sheep, a couple of pigs. There was always something happening

RIGHT: Gerald Armstrong seemed all right when I arrived in Middleham. He looked a whizzo old man really

RIGHT: I didn't exactly go for driving lessons – it was more a case of nicking a car and belting along the lanes around Middleham

ABOVE: That's John Forbes on the left next to Dougy Armstrong and me on the right with my Elvis Presley haircut. We became great mates and still are. The three musketeers. The other lad is Buck McMahon who had ridden a winner so we respected him

BELOW: I used to get around a bit even though I was small. We went out to a cafe in Middleham to play pinball and listen to records

RIGHT: I hadn't realised at first that I wouldn't see my parents for the best part of a year. After that they came down to Middleham a lot and were always very supportive

BELOW: The first horse I ever looked after was Marija. I am working her here alongside Charlie Brown. She was a silly old cow, but of course I got fond of her, and she was my first ride in public. We finished last

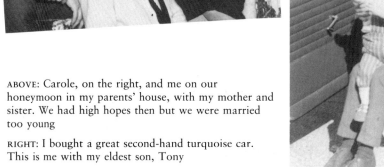

ABOVE: Carole, on the right, and me on our honeymoon in my parents' house, with my mother and sister. We had high hopes then but we were married too young

RIGHT: I bought a great second-hand turquoise car. This is me with my eldest son, Tony

BELOW: An early winner at Haydock on one of Ernie Weymes's horses

BELOW: Sam thought the world of his boys and would go through fire for them. The Armstrong family are me. They are my success.

ABOVE: Everybody was so smart in Newmarket. Everything was cleaner and the strings were so much larger. You could notice the wealth difference

RIGHT: Lord Derby said I would have a house to go with the job. I got Falmouth Cottage. It wasn't a house, it was a mansion

RIGHT: When Laureate had won at Thirsk I'd thrown away my crutches. In the Derby he was my first Classic ride. This is us winning the Lingfield Derby trial

BELOW: Lady Derby was a great girl. She came down to stable lads talk and would always make me feel at ease

BELOW RIGHT: Lord Derby was aristocracy and one of the top men in the hierarchy. When I saw him it was always very formal

BELOW: I got on all right with the kids. I enjoyed them just like anyone else. It wasn't obvious at the time but I was being torn away from family life

BOTTOM: High Top's Guineas. I could hear this horse behind and it wasn't making any progress. My first Classic. I'd done it. It was just marvellous

RIGHT: Bernard was part of my education. The last of the gentleman trainers. He was quite a card

it. One jockey, Lance Harvey, wanted to take his tack with him but I told him to leave it. So we chucked our tack in a box and went. There were about ten of us in one taxi. We stayed back at the hotel and only heard later what had happened.

They had absolutely wrecked the whole course, set fire to it, and stabbed the clerk of the course. I don't know for how long racing was stopped – I didn't stay to find out – but they had to dig up the track and re-turf it. The riot was reputed to have been political, the horses just an excuse. They had stopped cars on the sides of the roads, siphoned out the petrol and set fire to them.

After the riot I was on the first plane. I couldn't wait to get out of it. There was a funny story afterwards. Brian Taylor, the jockey who'd been beaten in the second, was rung up by Barney Woods, who had lived in India for a few years and could do the accent. He said to Brian, 'We're going to get you because you know you pulled our horse up today. We are really going to get you, you bastard.' Then he rang him again and Brian took him so seriously that he got on a plane that night to Bombay, leaving his missus and kids behind. He said he had to be in Bombay to ride the next day.

You're not allowed to bring any rupees out of India so what you earned there you had to spend. It was a working holiday. I think I still have a bit of money sitting out there. I don't suppose I'll be getting interest on it. You couldn't make a lot of money, just enough to survive on and go out to dinner once a week. It was a way of life, though. It stopped you eating into your funds at home.

I rode one animal for Dinky, one of the top-priced yearlings, on its first run. It hadn't been showing a lot on the gallops but I gave it a ride and it finished third. Dinky wasn't happy because it had finished too close. The next time it ran it was wearing great big white bandages. It ran shocking, finished last. I was convinced there was something wrong with it. Dinky had packed those bandages solid, and I'm pretty sure he'd put padded lead in them. The horse won afterwards.

Sometimes Dinky would get himself into a muddle. He was

the sort of guy who could tell you about everyone else's horses but not his own. Gradually I started to lose the rides on his horses and by the end I wouldn't have gone back the following year. Before I left I'd started to get rides from other people and to ride winners, but I didn't set the world on fire. The horses are very different over there and they're trained rather differently from ours. I think they get a bit fed up. I remember riding an old character who pulled hard. I'd had a party the night before and after I'd ridden him I felt yucky. It wasn't incredibly hot though, because you rode in the mist in the morning – it was always misty before the sun came up and the sunrise was really beautiful.

In December 1971 I went to Calcutta to ride in the 2,000 Guineas. They wanted me to ride the horse and to stay in India but I said I couldn't. I'd been voted Jockey of the Year. That was a really big thing for me and I wasn't going to miss the award. So I said, right, the race is on Saturday and the awards are on Monday, so there's plenty of time.

I was staying on my own in a new hotel. And war broke out. There were blackouts. The phone rang at about three in the morning. It was Carole. She said, 'Are you all right?' I said, 'Of course I'm all right.' She said, 'There's a war on there.' She'd been panicking about it. I said, 'Of course there's a war on, oh go to sleep.' And I put the phone down because I wanted to get back to sleep. The war was only forty-five miles away but it didn't seem like a war. Life was going on as normal in Calcutta, except for some activity at the army camp where they were flying in the wounded.

Then the race was put back a day because Mrs Ghandi was coming to talk to the people. It must have been an amazing sight because I think the whole of India came to see her. Black heads and white clothes, such an incredible sight: all the green disappeared from this vast area.

I had worked out that I could ride and still get on a flight home in time. We raced the next day and I finished second to Dennis Ryan. That was the first disappointment. Then that afternoon they closed the airport: MIGs were coming in and out, filling up and going off again, and civilian aircraft weren't allowed. I couldn't go home.

I got on the first plane out on the Sunday evening, to Bombay. A racing fan called BJ Gould was assigned to look after me. He went with me to make sure I got on the first flight out of Bombay to London. It was due out six hours later, after dark. They had blackouts in Bombay as well.

On the way to the airport that night there was an air raid. All the traffic stopped and everybody began shouting and screaming. Where there were lights on in the town people were kicking and bashing with sticks to smash the lights and screaming at houses that weren't blacked out. It was pandemonium. And I could see a fire starting. I thought we were being bombed. Then I saw BJ with a handkerchief stuffed in his mouth, shaking with fear, virtually crying. I got out of the car, on to the pavement and behind a wall. BJ was lying on the pavement. I was looking over, watching, and I was petrified. I was in a war. We were getting shot at. And all this banging, the sky like Guy Fawkes night, red with tracers. Then there was a plane coming, straight for us. A tracer went past my ear and about three seconds later I was on the other side of the wall.

I jellied. My pants weren't too good. I could see my fear more than some of the others, though. They were really panicking. I couldn't believe it. And I realised then that I wouldn't want to go to war with an Indian.

When it had all died down we dusted ourselves off, got back in the car and drove to the airport. There were dead bodies on the road, people lying in the gutter, and nobody bothered. Later, when I got back to England, I found out that sixteen people had been killed.

I was lucky to get a place on the plane that night. There were a lot of other people wanting to get on, too. But I had a bit of a connection and I made it. At the airport we were told there was a bomber coming, but it turned out to be a false alarm. We took off with only a little blue-purple light on the runway. And we had to keep all the shades down on the plane. The pilot told us we would be taking off in the dark and going out to sea. After twenty minutes it would be all right. It wasn't. I remember sitting in that plane as it took off. It was very, very quiet. And it stayed very, very quiet. Eventually we were out of range, then it was all right.

All I was thinking about was getting home for my champion jockey award. When we landed I was nearly first off the plane. When the door opened at Heathrow it was amazing: TV cameras galore, and I had to do an interview about the state of the war in India. War correspondent!

8

WORKING TO BE CHAMPION

The longest shadow, that's what Lester cast. He had been a boy wonder when he won his first Derby on Never Say Die in 1954 and by the sixties he was in his prime. Nijinsky's Derby in 1970 was his fifth. He was in a run of eight consecutive jockeys' titles. He had champions right back through his pedigree. He had always seemed on a different planet to W. Carson.

In something as scrutinised as the racing circus, everyone gets put into a pecking order. The difficulty is in improving your position. Carson was on the ladder all right. But he was seen as a tireless little trier. Not as a big-race pilot. Changing ourselves as others see us is not an easy trick. Especially if you have already got further than anyone, including yourself, had ever imagined.

At this stage Willie was seen as something more than just a lightweight but still not a true big-race jockey. His whole attitude to life, even his style of riding, was too unpretentious for that. He had no family racing connections, indeed there had been no meteoric young apprentice start, very much the reverse. So when challenged as to his hopes at this stage he would shrug away suggestions of titles. 'I just keep pushing,' he said. And he did so to such an extent that he began to become a presence you wanted on your side.

Other pros began to shake their heads in acknowledgement. There was a degree of mockery, too. 'What's that?' he was asked down at the start of a Newmarket event for unraced two-year-olds. Willie didn't know, didn't mind, he was going to give it his best anyway. And that best had already become something the others couldn't do. 'It's odd,' said the now sadly deceased Tony Murray at the time, 'but Willie seems to get them relaxed by pushing at them. You will see him beginning to pump a long, long way out. He's not in trouble, he's just beginning to get them to run. And he's so fit that he can keep upping and upping the tempo all the way to the line. The rest of us couldn't do that.'

So Carson had become a method. The little urging figure clamped tight in behind the mane, building and building the effort as the winning post came at him. When a jockey is special there becomes an inevitability about a finish. A tangible sense of him and his horse being hungry for the line. Again and again the little Scottish blitzkrieg would grab it at the death. He began to be a very bad man to be in against your money. We began to reconsider his rating. So did he.

For here was a natural competitor. As success came, ambition grew. Why should he accept second best? To anyone?   U

L ester Piggott kept riding all the good horses. I had a few disappointments. I was going to get the ride on Park Top one day at Brighton. Piggott wasn't available and it was between Geoff Lewis and myself. Bernard didn't give me the ride because Park Top had ten stone to carry. If she hadn't had all that weight, I might have got the job. Then, of course, Geoff Lewis made a balls-up and was given the heave-ho, and Piggott got on her. I rode Park Top only once at home. Bernard never asked me to ride her because I wasn't going to ride her in a race, which was quite fair.

I may not have been riding horses as good as Park Top but I had come a long way from the likes of Marija. I was starting to get on the brink of riding a horse that could really gallop properly. And the more success I had, the more confidence I developed in my own ability, something I never had before. I was still the best lightweight but then I realised I wanted to be better than that. It was after quite a lot of success, around champion jockey time, that I started to let my weight go up. There was no longer any need to keep it down.

Things kept getting better during 1970, but there was no explosion. It was just another rung on the ladder. I was still working very hard, going anywhere and riding anything.

Sunday mornings were the big thing in those days. You sat by the telephone, hoping, willing it to ring, because when it rang on Sunday morning it was a trainer wanting to book you. There was very little going on abroad on Sundays in those days so everybody sat down and did their bookings for the whole week. I'd be sitting by the phone with pen in hand and calendar ready, marked up with my retained horses and the ones I would probably be asked to ride again – you had an idea of what you'd get – and just willed that phone to ring.

I did all that myself until Ted Eley took over as my agent. Ted knew every owner, every horse. He was a racing nut. He could tell you everything. We became friendly and I took him on to help me with my rides. I was one of the first jockeys to have an agent. Instead of waiting for people to ring up we decided to do what Lester was doing: ringing people up and asking to ride their horses. And we were quite successful.

By that time I was only losing the top rides to Lester. Bernard was starting to go to France a lot and Lester got all those horses as I wasn't very experienced in Europe, although I had started going to Sweden on Sundays. It was quite fun getting away from home. When Bernard went to France he always went overnight, because he liked his gambling. When I started to go with him I would stay in the motel and after dinner he'd tuck me up then go out gambling.

I was still in a master-servant relationship with Bernard. Although I was close to him he was still very much the master. He was a man that I admired and I would do anything for him because I knew that he would keep me straight. He was my god in a way and he was very fair. I knew he had my interests at heart. We became a team.

As I say, he was a real gambler. There was nothing he loved more than to pull a stroke. It gave him a real kick. Everyone knows the Old Lucky story: he had had three quiet runs, and I'd done my best on him last time out and he'd got beat so I didn't think he'd be good enough to win the Hunt Cup. But Bernard was cleverer than me. He'd been training the horse for the race. He laughed at me in the paddock beforehand when I said I didn't think he'd win. And of course the horse had improved from that race and pissed up. One of the press said, 'Well, Bernard, what's the plan for this horse?' And he said, 'Well, my dear boy, that *was* the plan.'

I used to crick my neck in the paddock just looking up at Bernard because he was six foot two. It's funny but I've seldom been aware of my smallness. I nearly always feel normal. It doesn't matter if I'm with tall people or not, it never really worries me.

Another time I was going down to Brighton with Bernard on the Pullman, the *Brighton Belle*. We were talking about the horse I was going to be riding for him and I said that the biggest problem would be not winning too far. He said, 'Yes, you're right,' and told me his plans for the horse. I'd just had a four-day suspension and this was my first race back. In the race I did look like winning too far, so I dropped my hands and there was a photo finish. I thought, oh shit, and took extra time pulling up so that the result would be out before I got back. I was praying that I'd won. I had, a short head. That really amused Bernard. He was laughing, joking, he really loved it. But I'm sure if I'd got back before the result had been out, there would have been problems. He wouldn't have lost his temper because he didn't do that, he just went cold, quiet and terse.

At the start of 1971 he had some good horses – High Top, Sharpen Up – but it was always said that they were getting a lot of help from the shoes. There was a lot of controversy over the shoes Bernard used. They were American style, with toe grabs. They did make a lot of difference. It was like me running with spikes and the others running with flat shoes. It became illegal. Bernard was always being told to file them down. I suppose they were a bad thing, because if you'd struck into another horse you'd have ruined it. And in Britain horses do slip up more round turns, so it's more dangerous.

Tony Murray was a big pal of mine. In a sense we went for the championship together. We used to go to the races together and talk about flaming Piggott a lot. That was the big thing. In a sense we were fighting one another, but we were also pretenders trying to topple the greats – a year before, people had never even heard of me.

Tony and I were really obsessed by Lester. It was the only thing we ever talked about. I was told it was possible that he could be toppled. Lester chose to ride more abroad and to scale down a bit. He was going to little meetings just to ride the 'good things'. So we could see a little chink of light at the end of the tunnel and we were going for it as hard as we could.

Lester's phoning around for rides was upsetting. I always wondered why people were in such awe. I was a bit that way myself at one time. It always amazed me how he could manipulate so much. If the trainer wouldn't let him on the horse he would ring the owner. I never confronted him about it though, because we were all in the same game together and it was all fair in love and war, as it were.

I think he was always quite fair in a race, though he wouldn't make things easy for you. Because of the cameras and everything being filmed, people 'doing' one another was becoming a thing of the past. Nowadays it might happen through an accident or carelessness – in the old days it was deliberate.

In 1971 Lester was still unreal. He had a great racing brain, and his finger was always on the pulse. He had that uncanny knack of knowing how to beat you. He would get the best out of his own horse. That was his secret. It was his dedication to knowing all the opposition. He knew what to do. He knew what was best for his horse and he knew the worst of the others, and that won him races. And he was always slick, steady and smooth through a race, never panicked. He was strong and determined in a finish, though of course we did beat him on occasions.

He was very hard to beat, though. He seemed to have all the ammunition. When we did beat him it was glory, hallelujah. When he made a mistake, chose the wrong one or whatever, it was good. But he was like the Berlin Wall: to begin with you were up against it, and only gradually did you start breaking it down. That was a bit of his own doing of course, because he began to go abroad. He had a real stranglehold on racing.

It was said that Piggott rode a fantastic race on The Minstrel in the Derby. He won the race, but so he should have done. He was on The bloody Minstrel, for goodness sake, and he only beat Hot Grove a neck. Hot Grove was out of a hurdler. Lester was sitting on a Group One horse who went on to win the

King George. Course he should have won. Hot Grove ran the race of his life. I kicked on very early that day because I knew I was on a horse that got a mile and a half and that was my only chance of winning. So I kicked early and some people say I completely ballsed it up. Nobody ever said that Lester nearly ballsed it up, gave his horse too much to do, gave me too much leeway, none of that was said. But then winning is everything.

I didn't really have much of a relationship with Lester socially. I didn't hate him, I admired him, as we all do. I hated him as a competitor but I really admired him so much. There's a hell of a lot in him that I'd like to be. Not all of it but a lot. He *is* mean, but I think he's gone that way because people have sent him that way. He's played on it. It's a game. You'd go to the races with him, buy him an ice cream and never get the money. So you only did it a couple of times and the third time it was 'get it your bloody self'.

At the end of one race he was in third and he shouted, 'Five hundred, five hundred, five hundred,' and I let him pass. Of course, he never meant it. So when he did it again I told him to piss off. I would never do anything he told me to. He was a bit clever like that, you know. He shouts at you in the race, just to get your attention.

I always had rows with him afterwards in the weighing room. He once said I couldn't ride a bike. When things haven't gone quite right for him he gets very annoyed. I used to laugh at him. I still do. What else can you do? You can't take it too seriously.

Once at Ascot he beat me a short head and he said, 'Got you, ha ha ha.' I went, 'Well done, you old bastard,' and hit him over the head with the whip. It wasn't malicious, we weren't fighting, but for some reason the stewards thought we were always at loggerheads. Maybe it was just his rivalry against me, maybe I was frightening him.

There was one day at Windsor when I was riding a filly for Barry Hills which had been second three times. It was the evening after the big Goodwood meeting and Lester had ridden nine winners, won all the big races, had a fantastic week. He came over by helicopter, had a glass of champagne on the way. He had been resting that day, been in the sauna, and the champagne went to his head and he was feeling a bit joyous. I came upside him at the furlong pole and was going better than him. I didn't say anything to him. He must have looked at me and could see that he wasn't going to win, and he pushed me. It gave me a shock. I lost my balance and nearly fell off. It was the will to win. He's got that funny devil thing about him. He did it to get the edge. I still won, which was just as well. There were no cameras in those days. If it had been a camera job like nowadays, he would have been in serious trouble. He went into the stewards' room and said it was his whip action or something that had caught me. The stewards took a dim view. I think I cooled it a bit in front of them. I didn't say too much. But they saw it, they didn't need me to tell them, and he got a dressing down. Then off he went.

I think it worried me a bit then, but I've lived under his shadow all my life and it doesn't bother me. It's the press that have made Piggott fantastic. I was always nice to the press – until I got problems with Dick Hern – always laughing and joking, talking to everybody. The press say I'm terse, not always helpful, and yet Piggott won't even talk to them. He tells them to bog off, and he's a hero. And they have made him that way. Lester always had their backing. If he made a mistake, it was because he meant to. It was always different with him somehow.

I've always been open, always told the truth. Even the stewards can't get over that: they don't believe me because they think I'm telling lies. That's life, I suppose. You tell the truth all the time and people think it's not right because sometimes the truth hurts. But Piggott, he's got a mystique about him, the unknown. He wouldn't talk, nobody got to know him. Nobody gets to know him because he's a strange creature. Even today, who knows him? He still has that magic mystique which makes him unusual.

I never had a fight with him, although in the weighing room people did occasionally stand up to one another. Eric Eldin took a race off me in the stewards' room at Brighton one day. He said I'd bumped him or something. Maybe he thought I had but I never touched him. That sort of thing did happen in those days. You would only have to go near a horse and they could say, 'He slammed into me,' and the stewards disqualified you. I was annoyed but I didn't hit him. I was too small to hit anybody.

I've never seen a real fight between jockeys. You see them sparring, wrestling, rather than hitting. Except once at Newmarket. Lester believed that Geoff Baxter had annoyed him going down to the start and so he had a go at Geoff and hit him with his stick. Geoff said, 'What did you do that for?' Lester said, 'You annoyed me.' Geoff insisted that Lester apologise but Lester wouldn't. The race was run and Geoff came into the weighing room, put his saddle down, walked up to Lester and tapped him on the shoulder. As Lester turned Geoff whacked him right in the jaw, and down Lester went. Geoff said to him when he was down, 'Apologise!' Lester was so shocked he couldn't move. To his credit, he pulled himself up and said to little Des Cullen, his valet at the time, 'You were supposed to protect me, you were!' The first I heard about it all was in the loo when Lester came in nursing his jaw.

1971 was the year when we had seventeen individual two-year-old winners. One of them was Crowned Prince, which I was never going to ride. He was the most expensive yearling bought at sale at that time. Lovely-looking horse, great big powerful chestnut. Bernard told me right from the start that I wouldn't be riding the horse and that Lester would be retained to ride him. It never really worried me. Bernard was straight right from the word go, very fair, but then he always was. This horse looked magnificent, the most beautiful racehorse you could ever wish to see, and with a lovely character. And I never even sat on him. There might have been a reason. Bernard was always protective of me and perhaps he thought I was better off out of it really.

I rode all the others, and in fact it ended up well for me. I was riding High Top and Sharpen Up. Sharpen Up won for the first time at Nottingham, with Piggott. I chucked Lester off later and then Sharpen Up was mine. That was when the dreams were coming true: riding proper horses like that. I couldn't believe it really. To be champion jockey. . .

In 1972 I won my first Classic, the 2,000 Guineas on High Top. My first Classic: I'd done it. It was just marvellous. I had done what Bernard had told me to do. He was always telling me what to do, which of the other horses to track, which ones to watch out for. High Top was a strong horse – he just ran away with me going to post. There was a bloody howling wind blowing across the course, the rain was lashing down. High Top was in front, and at the furlong pole I thought, 'No, he's gone.' Then I could hear this horse coming behind me and it wasn't making any progress. Fantastic. Bernard had tears in his eyes. He had suffered the disappointment of Crowned Prince going wrong. And I, the jockey that hadn't been allowed to ride the wonder horse, had won the Guineas on the other one, which was quite marvellous. Unfortunately that was the last race he ever won. It was Bernard's first and only Classic winner.

1972 was when Tony Murray and I were battling for the championship, struggling for more winners which weren't coming all that quickly. We were nip and tuck for a long time and it could have gone either way. I had a bad fall in August, fractured my cheekbone. At the time it looked as though that was it. I remember being nearly in tears in hospital, thinking that I was going to lose it because of a fall. It was on the old seven furlong course at York. I was riding a horse for Clive Brittain, they closed on me a bit, I clipped the hedge and down I went. I was kicked in the face. My cheek was smashed in but I had an operation in which they stuck a skewer in and pulled the bone back into position and then it was all right. I rode again four days later. It was awfully sore. Black and blue.

The championship was quite close right up to the end of the season. Then I pulled away a bit. I'd done it. I was champion jockey. I was exhausted at the end of it. I'd put a lot into it, travelled everywhere. Anywhere there was a ride I would go. I put my heart and soul into getting there. At the end of the season I virtually slept for three days. I did get up during the day but I was barely conscious. I was drained. The adrenalin had stopped running.

I gave a party at the Woodlands Hotel, just outside

Cambridge. I sat eighty people down to dinner and I gave a little toast: 'It's been my year, now it's your night.' People had gone to a lot of trouble: when I arrived at the Woodlands they had put 'Well Done Champion Jockey' on the doorway in a horseshoe.

9
CELEBRITY

He was a breath of fresh air. The little pleased-to-see-you Scotsman who seemed as happily surprised at his own success as anyone. Suddenly there was a new big name on the block. Someone from outside the magic circle who was proud to tell his story but wouldn't bog you down with claims to greatness. The scrapbook at this time is full of copy from feature writers captivated by the down-to-earth ethic of Willie, agent Ted Eley, wife Carole and the boys.

It's worth stressing the scrapbook. Fame is the spur in racing, too. And for the young apprentice that just means having your name in the paper. Looking back at May Carson's scrapbook, you can see the excitement in the few lines cut out of the *Scottish Daily Mail* in June 1963: 'Stirling born Billy Carson returned to his native Scotland to ride a winner at Ayr yesterday.' Those things are truly treasured. Because at the time they may be the last.

So for the teenage hopeful the racing press begin by being remote fantasy figures. They had ringing 1920s names: Captain Heath, The Scout, Gary Owen. They had an almost magical power. They could put YOU in the paper. At the start, if they call, you are ALWAYS available.

There is a rather unfeeling casualness about the way the press pick up an apprentice and then drop him once he seems to have outlived his first 'dream debut' headlines. There is always another one to write about. Last year's boy wonder is no longer news. And anyway, his prowess was probably as much due to the publicity from the press as from any innate title-seeking talent. The facts are that a Flat-race jockey can perform with the best right into his fifties. Almost as long as a bank clerk. Take the swift mathematics and you see that the top ten riders will take only three or four recruits a decade. Not many boy wonders in that.

But Willie was never an overnight star. Quite the reverse. He had made the slowest start of any champion jockey in history.

Just twenty-two winners by the time he was twenty-one. There had been no instant early romance with the press. Just slightly patronising mentions of the wee lad from Stirling who was doing the best he could and proud to talk about it. But then he hit the big time and was still the same. Still busy and laughing and proud and unpretentious. That's when the media romance began. As always it was a dangerous game.

Willie was not often emotional when he talked about the book but this was a watershed. There was a certain wistfulness as he looked back and recognised the changes in him. Now he is a long-proven champion in his field. A property owner and a millionaire in his own right, and very conscious of how he has had to work to get it. He couldn't remember one candid remark in the exhausted wake of his first title: 'I was happy just jogging along,' he had said to me at the time, 'but Carole kept badgering me to put myself about. I didn't really want to be champion jockey.'

But it had happened. The world's press, or at least a sizeable chunk of the British sporting section, were at the Carsons' door. And the Carsons invited the monsters in. Life was public now. Happily or unhappily, it was bound to be different. ∪

It wasn't obvious at the time, but I was being torn away from family life. My career has always come first.

I didn't do much philosophising on life. I was busy doing my own thing, I wasn't worrying about what my family were doing. They were getting fed and looked after and I thought I was doing a good job. Now I can see a lot of wrongs in it. But at the time I didn't see it that way. The kids went to the convent school. I got on all right with them. I enjoyed them just like anybody else, but didn't want too much of them. There were no real hassles.

In 1973 I was made a freeman of Stirling. And then there was *This Is Your Life*. I thought beforehand there was something fishy going on. Carole would put the phone down when I came in and there were other little things that just didn't seem right. I sensed that she was up to no good but I didn't know what. Then one morning Ted said he was taking the kids off to the zoo. Carole went to get her hair done and there was only me in the house. I thought there was something funny going on then because normally there was always somebody in the house. Carole always had someone round for coffee and a chat. But that day, nothing. In the evening we were due to go down to the Sportsman's Club because they wanted to give me an award or some such thing.

I was sitting there at home on my own and I got the invitation out: dinner jacket, 6.30. It seemed a funny time. So I picked the phone up and rang the Sportsman's Club. It was lucky that I got the right person who clicked straight away and played me along. If I'd got anybody else, they would have said, 'Oh yeah, they're doing *This Is Your Life* here, the cameras are round the back and all the guests are arriving.'

Anyway, I drove up to Tottenham Court Road and somebody was there to take my car. I thought that was a bit odd. As we walked up this man said, 'Just hang on a second will you,' and made up some cock-and-bull story. I had to wait on the stairs of the reception area before going up. I remember thinking to myself: this is the sort of thing that happens on *This Is Your Life*. I went upstairs and they put this ruddy trophy in my hands and the photographers were all saying, 'Smile at the camera, sir.' Cheeky sods. And then Eamonn Andrews came in and stood beside me and said, 'This Is Your Life'. I said, 'Bloody hell, I'm not old enough.' I had to do a speech.

The programme played on the fact that I was the man who was upstaging Piggott. I can't say I enjoyed it. I found it embarrassing. I suppose really if you had a choice you would say, 'No thanks'. Everybody else seemed to enjoy it, but it just seemed a bit tacky, people coming in and talking about you. They only ever say the good things, never the bad ones. I was only a kid after all.

Suzanne Kane came on the scene due to the Barry Hills connection. She was working at his stable as an amateur rider and I was spending quite a lot of time riding horses there and staying with Barry and Maureen.

Suzanne wasn't the first. I'd been casually active. There was a girlfriend in the north – that was all, it was never going to be anything serious. I think Carole suspected. She was always ringing up at night trying to find out where I was. It all started in the late sixties, hence my discussion with Lord and Lady Derby. In all fairness, Carole and I were growing apart. I wanted to better myself and she was happy just plodding along. In her eyes, she had come a long way already, given her background. I had been having dinners with Bernard van Cutsem, been involved with aristocracy, seen what they did, and I presume I thought that was the way to go. I wanted to improve and she didn't and I think that's where the differences started.

There were always arguments about the boys' schooling, too. I wanted to send them to boarding school, both because I wanted to be more middle class and because I could see that it was the right thing for them. I could see that people went through life better if they had an education and I wanted that for my kids. But Carole wouldn't let me.

The split-up was a gradual thing, but it was a bit nasty at the end. When it all broke the paparazzi were after me everywhere, wanted to know everything. They sat outside Suzanne Kane's parents' house in Kingston. We didn't know what to do. Lilian, Suzanne's mother, was a good driver and had a Mini Cooper. So we got in it and drove out of the drive past the waiting photographers. Suzanne was in the back and I was in the front and we went towards London. We had a race, trying to get rid of them. The little Mini Cooper was going pretty quick, but we still couldn't lose them. I was telling Lilian what to do, where to go. Then I had an idea. 'Go to Harrods and I'll meet you at the hairdressers.' I jumped out of the car, ran straight through Harrods, out of the back door and away. And I lost them. They were parked outside my home for a week, just sitting there.

After that, everything I did got into the press because I was doing things that were not socially normal. In their eyes I was newsworthy. If I walked into an airport, they all took pictures. Now I walk in past the same photographers and say 'Hello, boys', but they don't want my picture any more.

I left home and went to stay with Suzanne at her house in Lambourn. Then Carole moved out of the house in

Newmarket so Suzanne and I went to live there. Meantime Carole had bought the house at St Marina, down the road, and moved in with someone who had been a lodger of mine. I remember her telling me that she hadn't been a saint before I left anyway.

Anybody who has been separated can tell you that it's a very tiring time emotionally. It's not something I'd want to go through again. I didn't explain it to the kids at all. They were upset. I spoke to them on the phone and they asked when I was coming home, normal things that kids would say to their father. I suppose I fobbed them off with a story. I wasn't going to promise them anything.

I saw Suzanne as a vehicle of improvement for myself. She was educated and there was a lot about her that could educate me. She taught me a lot: how to behave, how to speak – I still had my Scottish accent. I didn't have much education and although I'd been involved with aristocracy I wasn't close to them.

Suzanne was a very unfortunate person: she had epilepsy and didn't always make sense. But she was very kind and good hearted. She didn't get on with my kids at all, though. We tried but it didn't work. She was not a person that got on with kids all that well. She was all right with them for a while but not every day.

Financially, Carole screwed me. She went for what she could. Maybe she was right. But it knocked me seriously. I got divorced at the wrong time, when the law favoured the woman. I didn't mind providing for the children but she ended up with half of everything. I had to start building up funds all over again. It was a terrible time. It set me back emotionally more than anything. You don't know who your friends are, that's the trouble. You really don't know who to turn to. It's something that nobody should go through.

I started to mix with a new set of people, Suzanne's friends. I enjoyed the London scene: nightclubs, dinners, going to all the bistros. I've still got a lot of friends from that time. They were all young people working in the city. Suzanne made me more fashionable, told me that flower power had died and all my old stuff had to go. There was nobody else to show me –

Carole didn't know. I've never really worried about clothes. I've always allowed the womenfolk to worry about it. I've never been what you'd call a snappy dresser. Suzanne used to take me to Harrods boys' department because there was no VAT on children's clothes. We got cashmere sweaters for me there. My hairstyle changed too. No more short back and sides. I went to a fellah on Brompton Road, a shop called Smile.

The London scene didn't interfere with my riding because we used Suzanne's parents' house as a base, which was quite convenient. Her father was a bit of a strange character. The family had made money out of the pneumatic drill – the great-grandfather had invented it. The grandmother owned a horse with Dick Hern, Southern Rose, which I bred for her.

Occasionally I suppose I felt I was being patronised because I was just a jockey, but I didn't let it worry me. It was a changing world, working-class people were becoming respectable. We were never going to be married. Suzanne was hopeful, but I kept telling her she had to change before I'd marry her. She was too crazy, too outspoken, a bit of an oddball. I enjoyed it all to begin with, but then I got a bit bored. And her epilepsy, which had started after a fall, wasn't getting any better. But she opened up a new way of life for me, one that I hadn't seen before.

10
PROFESSIONAL GRADING

By 1975 Willie Carson had succeeded beyond his wildest dreams. If the tiny teenager facing that daunting Middleham snowstorm had been told that eighteen years later he would have already been champion jockey twice, he would have thought he'd been into *Rainbow Jacket* daydreams at the cinema. What would have been beyond any comprehension would have been that, in career terms, he hadn't got halfway.

In hindsight the logic is obvious. At the time it wasn't, mainly because Willie was still underrated by many people, not least himself. At this stage we all recognised his exceptional talents of energy and inspiration but there was still a tendency to underrate him as a big-race jockey. 'Brute force and ignorance' was the disparaging comment attributed to John Sharratt, *Raceform*'s most respected observer. It was probably a selective quotation but it reflected a widespread view. Willie Carson represented sweat and endeavour, journeyman's values. It was easy to pigeon-hole him there. But it was wrong.

All that was needed was a bit of lateral thinking. Willie was already champion and had youth on his side. In his own way he was obviously ambitious for more. He was ready not just for the hustle jobs but for a big team. If you were around the racing circus and you were a lateral thinker, the elements could be put together. In all Britain, let alone just in the little racing show, there are few better brains than Arnold Weinstock. Besides his great industrial success with GEC, he now owned West Ilsley Stables in Berkshire, at that stage the premier private training operation out of Newmarket. He was looking to the future.

'The trick is to find people with both talent and incentive,' Lord Weinstock says, looking back down the years in that measured Solomon's way of his. 'Willie represented both. He was already champion but was still in his early thirties. If we took him then, we would have him at the peak of his powers.

In my judgement many jockeys go on getting the credit when their ability is already on the wane.' At this distance, that statement rides over the storm which blew up when the news came out in midsummer that Joe Mercer was to be replaced next season. Passions ran high; looking back, the cuttings have the familiar aggrieved look, if not quite the revolutionary rumblings of the Queen's handling of Dick Hern and the Nashwan affair twelve years later.

Joe Mercer was a fixture at West Ilsley. He had first gone there for the then trainer Jack Colling when still a nineteen-year-old apprentice in 1953. He had won the Oaks on Ambiguity in that opening season and in the years that followed became established as the classic stylist amongst the riding ranks. Success continued and grew when Dick Hern took over the West Ilsley operation and culminated in Brigadier Gerard's record achievements in 1971 and 1972. There had been two Classics for the Queen with Highclere in 1974, a record-breaking Coronation Cup with Bustino in 1975. In view of the lucrative Indian summer to Carson's career (his highest-earning years were in his late forties) it is ironic to note that age was amongst the reasons for Mercer's replacement. In 1976 he was just forty-two.

But Weinstock had made his judgement and for Carson it was a case of continuing to adjust his sights upwards. In this sense a top jockey is like a star striker in soccer. He needs to keep improving his game. But he must also make judgements on the team which is supposed to supply the passes. No service, no goals. A jockey's own development will not necessarily be matched by the stable for which he rides.

The readjustments required are difficult, diplomatic and sometimes simply sad. For Willie, it was very obviously the latter. Bernard van Cutsem was dying of cancer.　　　U

The last time I saw Bernard I was going off to Hong Kong. He had been in hospital and I knew he wasn't well. I'd been away for the whole winter and hadn't seen him for a while so I thought I'd better go round. I was led in by the chauffeur, who was looking after him. He was sitting in his study. He looked frail, so frail. It really shocked me. I became so embarrassed because I couldn't understand what he was saying. He was trying to talk to me but they had taken his voice-box away. So he started to write it down. He wrote: 'I won't need you to ride for me next year.' I remember my heart thumping. And then I heard this sort of laughter, a gurgling and spluttering noise, and he wrote: 'because I am only seven stone seven myself.' He was chuckling with a liquid sort of noise, trying to laugh.

I never saw him again. I didn't know then that he was about to die. I wouldn't accept it. The news of his death came two weeks later. It was a very sad day, very sad indeed. He suffered a lot. I wished they had never done that operation on him, because he died anyway and he might have had a year's more normal life than he did. In that last year the charisma had gone from the yard because he was gone. I was still riding winners though there wasn't one special horse. Bernard was definitely going to be a big loss.

After his death I had an arrangement with Clive Brittain though, unknown to Clive, I had taken a retainer to be Dick Hern's jockey before Bernard died, in 1975.

Sir Gordon Richards had rung me up just before one of the Newmarket meetings and said he wanted to have a chat with me. He wouldn't have said too much because he was a little politician. He asked when could we meet, and could he come over to my house, so I said sure. I was still in Falmouth Cottage at the time. I was so excited: Sir Gordon Richards, the greatest jockey ever.

So, the great man turned up and we went into the study where we chatted for an hour and a half. When I went out to the car, I couldn't believe it: he'd left his wife sitting out there all that time. That annoyed me – she could have been inside having a cup of tea. Gordon was a bit funny that way. Anyway, we talked about whether I'd be interested in riding for Major Hern, who of course was training for Weinstock and Lady Beaverbrook at the time. Gordon was Lady Beaverbrook's racing manager.

Joe Mercer had been at West Ilsley before Dick Hern arrived. Dick sort of took him on with the stables. Jakie Astor owned the stables originally, then Weinstock bought them and so came to have the loudest say in what happened. He, for some reason, was not a fan of Joe Mercer, and was in favour of ousting him. I should think that Sir Gordon had stood up for Joe for quite a while, but I think most of the owners were very happy that Lord Weinstock preferred the change, for whatever reasons. That was why I was approached and of course I said I would be very interested indeed. I was told not to breathe a word and then later the deal was confirmed that I would start riding for them in two years time, at the beginning of 1977. It was all signed and sealed, and I had to say nothing. The Queen was always being mentioned: must keep quiet, mustn't embarrass Her Majesty the Queen. So I told nobody. I don't really know why they wanted the two-year gap. I think it was Lord Weinstock who was forcing the hand, but I have never asked Joe why there was a gap.

I was very happy. It was a big step for me. I was definitely bettering my career. I was walking into one of the top two stables of the time. The only thing that worried me was how I was going to break it to Bernard, who was obviously on the decline. In the end I never did get around to telling him that I was going to leave him.

I had the rest of 1975 to go through and the whole of the next season. But Clive Brittain kept approaching me to take a second retainer. I kept refusing and he kept offering a bit more. I kept saying no, because I knew it would only be for a year. But in the end it was getting harder to stop him constantly offering more, so I took it. That's how, when Bernard died, I ended up riding for Clive – he had a second claim on me. I think there was a time when Barry Hills had a second claim on me, too, but I was never his first jockey.

Then I was really dropped in the dirt. I went to Epsom and Dick Hern and Lord Porchester virtually grabbed me as soon as I arrived and ran me into an office. I wondered what I'd done. Were they going to cancel the deal? They said: 'Look, there's a problem, it looks as though the press have got hold of the news. Can you tell all your people straight away?' I said, 'What, now?' When I'd got my breath back I ran to poor Clive. I had wanted time to get people in the right mood, to tell them in my own way and explain my reasons. But I just had to get into the saddle and say, 'Oh, sorry Clive, but next year I won't be riding for you, I'll be riding for Dick Hern.' And I could see his face. Clive thought he had got me. He's ambitious and we would have made a very good team, he knew that. We were having a good time, things were going well and of course a top jockey riding for him would have attracted a bit of trade. The world was his oyster. Captain Marcos Lemos, Clive's main patron, wouldn't talk to me from then on because he was so disappointed. It was very nasty.

I had sat down and talked to Dick Hern about what we were going to do. I don't really know when Joe was told. In those times they were all pretty loyal: Porchester, Astor. But for some reason Lord Weinstock had a clash with Joe, and he was the big boss: it goes full circle, doesn't it? Eventually the Queen bought the place, became boss, and what did she do? Kicked people out. She kicked Dick Hern out. And you got more cries of indignation. It was the same thing with Joe Mercer being sacked after all those years there.

I felt sorry for Joe in a way. He must have been devastated. He couldn't have seen it coming. His relationship with Lord Weinstock couldn't have been that good, but his relationship with the Queen and Porchester and Astor and Dick was fabulous. He must have felt that he was in a concrete situation.

Rose Bowl was my best winner in 1975. I rode her after Lester had made a balls-up by waiting with her too long in the 1,000 Guineas. She won the Queen Elizabeth at Ascot and ended up over a mile and a quarter in the Champion. You had to be a bit patient riding her, only Lester exaggerated the tactics a bit. I've always been prone to going too soon. She had a tremendous turn of foot. I always said, until recently, that she was the best I'd ever ridden. She galloped like a deer – her back legs came in front of her.

My misfortune on Dibidale was the other notable event from this period. She had gone to the 1974 Oaks with a good chance. Barry Hills, her trainer, wasn't going to run her because of the firm ground, but it started to pour with rain the night before, which got me quite excited because I knew she'd have a chance.

I'm certain the girths were checked at the start; it's something I always do, have someone feel the girths. Dibidale was a very deep-girthed animal and you wouldn't have expected the saddle to move. In the race I was up in the first three going well, and then coming down the hill the reins started to get longer and her head further away from me. I didn't click until the saddle started to wobble and I felt a bit unsteady. I looked down and all I could see was chamois leather where the saddle should be. There I was about to come round Tattenham Corner doing a balancing act on her back. I thought I wasn't going to make it, so I worked my feet along until my toes were in the irons and kept my weight well balanced. Then I just left the saddle and jumped out of the irons on to her back. I remember thinking that I could still win. I took a bit of a battering riding bareback, the muscles get ripped about a bit, and I was sore between the legs. In the end Pat won and I was third. It wasn't until after I'd pulled up, with the help of Tony Murray, that I remembered the weightcloth and realised I'd get disqualified. I threw my stick on the ground in disgust.

11
WEST ILSLEY

Dick Hern was the number one. When Noel Murless retired in 1976 it was Dick who was recognised as the supreme master of the training profession. A shy, slightly deaf man in his mid-fifties, Major Hern kept a military bearing as well as the title. It made him seem a rather forbidding and aloof figure on a racetrack. Add to that the separateness of West Ilsley, the private training centre in Berkshire which Arnold Weinstock had just bought from Jakie Astor, and you got a touch of mystery about the man.

But there was nothing mysterious about the record. A horseman enough to have been an instructor at the then pre-eminent Porlock Riding School, Hern didn't take long to show the classy touch as a trainer. In 1958 he had joined the irascible Lionel Holliday and straight away turned out the Yorkshire Oaks winner, None Nicer. The next year he had the top-class sprinter Galivanter and when he won his first Classic with Hethersett's St Leger victory of 1962 it was the crowning achievement in his first season as champion trainer.

Taken to West Ilsley by Jakie Astor, he soon imposed unbeatable standards on what was a premier team. He won Classics with Provoke, and of course Highclere won the 1,000 Guineas and the French Oaks for the Queen. In the seventies he was seven times amongst the top five trainers and was clear champion in 1972 thanks to the peerless exploits of Brigadier Gerard. This was big time all right.

In every sense it was a new challenge for Willie Carson. Familiarity would be needed both for him and indeed for Dick Hern. But, for a while at least, this would be the best of times for both of them.   U

Being the Queen's jockey was a big thrill. When you put those colours on. . . . The first time I rode for her was at Wolverhampton, a horse called Christchurch. I was very, very proud to win on that. I already knew I had the job at Dick Hern's, and that was probably why I got the ride.

She came down to West Ilsley once, sometimes twice, a year. Nobody was told she was coming, though the Major knew two days beforehand. He might say, 'That Land-Rover's a bit dirty. Get it clean.' There were little signs like that and everybody would say, 'Oh-oh, Queen's coming.' He would ring me up the night before and say, 'Not to be repeated, but the Queen's arriving tomorrow.' But of course because of his habits everybody knew the night before anyway.

I remember one morning when I was living at East Ilsley I didn't hear the alarm, or it didn't go off. I was late. I had a Ferrari at the time and didn't that go down the road! The police wouldn't have caught me. When I got there the Queen had already arrived. Nobody said anything. I just filed in behind the rest.

She has so much on her mind and yet it's amazing how much knowledge she has. I find that with all the Royals. They retain a lot of information. She always talked about the breeding rather than the racing side of things. She remembered brothers and sisters. The brother did that, the mother won this. She really knew her families. She didn't need reminding about anything. In fact, she reminded us about a lot of things.

I suppose I started relaxing with her after I had had a few breakfasts with her and cracked a few jokes. I'd sit next to her and take the mickey out of everybody. Did she laugh? Sometimes. Not always. I remember a good remark she made when Dick was coming out with fancy ideas about new gallops and getting a bit more land. I said to her, 'Reach for your cheque book, Ma'am,' and she said, 'Yes, people are very free spending my money.' People always ask me what she's like. I say, she's like the Queen.

The best thing that happened to me in racing was winning the Oaks on Dunfermline for her. I was always a royalist and always will be.

I was given a retainer to ride the Queen's horses, including those at Ian Balding's: the mammoth sum of £1,000. Dick's retainer wasn't very good either, about £8,000, twice Bernard's. It wasn't a big sum even at that time.

Until I was given the job at West Ilsley I'd only really seen Dick on racecourses and I'd found him almost aloof. When he's on the course he's a man who goes about his own business, he's not much interested in anyone else and not a person you get to know very well. So I didn't know what to expect. I thought he'd be a very straight person, which he was. And I expected a regimental thing, too, which there was: very clear cut, very forthright, very loud in his orders. He knew what he was doing and because of the way he went about his business you felt he was definitely in command.

He had me down in West Ilsley pretty early in 1977, before March. I had had to give up Falmouth Cottage when I left van Cutsem and had lived in Eastbury until I left for Newbury. Looking for a house was a problem to begin with and involved discussion about my personal life. Being the Queen's jockey, my personal life was a major factor. It was put to me by Sir Gordon that I ought to be married. I think Suzanne had been asked to leave the room and he said, 'Are you going to marry this girl?' I think I gave a non-committal answer.

I suppose my relationship with Dick started off a bit master-and-servant, but it became more than that once I really got to know him and his wife. Sheilah would have me over for dinner and we became very friendly. After a while Dick became very friendly too. He learnt all about me and my ways. Everybody has their kinks and I suppose he learnt to trust me. I don't think he'd wanted to lose Joe Mercer but he accepted me very well. I was walking into a stable where no-one really wanted me and it was a bit tricky at first, but Dick and Sheilah, in all fairness to them, really made me welcome.

Lambourn was totally different from Newmarket and I found it difficult to adapt to begin with. I wasn't able to get the horses into my brain, what kind of horses they were. It was because we weren't going fast enough on the gallops. We were only cantering, then going half-speed and just letting them stretch to the finish. I felt as though I wasn't learning about the horses' characteristics. It's totally different in Newmarket, where you have to go faster to get the horses fit. The West Ilsley gallops were very strenuous for horses, they were working quite hard even though they weren't going that fast.

I had to learn the gallops. And the work jockeys helped a lot. When I first went there they were a first-rate staff, second to none, a highly skilled team. A new broom sweeps clean and I think they were chuffed to have got rid of Joe though they were reluctant to say so. And so to my surprise I actually felt as though I had them on my side right from the word go. They were always willing to tell me about the horses, whether they pulled early on and what have you. I remember they always said I wouldn't be able to ride one horse, Boldboy. He was a bit of a character. He was a bit savage in his box. They all said, 'You'll never be able to ride that, there's only one jockey who can ride that, Joe Mercer.' I won five races on him that year!

There were only about ten lads who rode regular work. They all did their three but Dick only allowed a certain number to ride work. So you would have four lots every morning going up galloping, sometimes five. It was all written down in advance and put up in the saddle room. So they knew when they got to the top which horse they were getting on, and which horse they were going behind. Then Dick would come and give the instructions. He'd ride down on his hunter and go along telling everybody what to do. By the time he'd finished we would be halfway down, walking, then he'd turn around and go back up to the top. He had three fences rigged up and he'd pop over them, just to keep his eye in – except when the ground was hard.

The lads were really good – some of them are still there. We had Stan Clayton, who was riding work then, and Harry Grant, who remembered me from Middleham. He was nicknamed The Old Whisperer. He was a great old boy. He rode very long and he smoked. When he saw the Guv'nor up front turning round he could get the end of the cigarette and take it into his mouth. The tip of his tongue would be in the tip of the cigarette. He used to ride Relkino all the time – and hold him. He kept riding out until he was nearly seventy.

Not all of the lads punted but they always knew when our horses were going to win. Only very rarely did one of ours slip the net. Sometimes I've known the lads to be the only ones who did know – even the trainer and the jockey didn't really. They would whisper afterwards that they had half-expected it to whiz in.

Dick knew I would have trouble learning the gallops. I remember being a bit confused because the way he did things was totally alien to me. It looked to me as if we were going up a mountain. I had virtually never been up a hill on the gallops in my life before. At Newmarket you go virtually half-pace from the start, and then not quite racing pace but getting that way. At Ilsley you cantered for the first two furlongs, absolutely cantered. It didn't feel like work. There I was struggling with these horses pulling. Then you went a little bit faster for the next two. And then, depending on what time of year it was and whatever you wanted to do with them, you let them run. But virtually the first half of the gallop was slow and there was never really a proper gallop in the Newmarket sense.

The maximum you could go on the winter gallops was seven furlongs. On the summer ones you could go further. A Derby horse would be trained more or less the same as all the others, except that just before Epsom Dick always cantered them a mile and a half on the round gallop, at a reasonable pace but fairly slow because you had to climb the hill. In very dry summers the all-weather chippings we had at Ilsley were used a lot. That's virtually six furlongs, up the hill, and you could always tell the horses that had been trained on it.

John Dunlop hasn't had a grass gallop for ten years. He has two all-weathers, one for cantering and one for working. There was one all-weather in Middleham, just a harrowed strip, dirt with stones and all sorts in it.

We started off on the right foot: my first ride was a winner. In fact I think the first eight runners we had were four winners and four seconds. Of course they were very fit. I soon realised that when his horses went racing they were there to race. Not like Newmarket horses, which had to get fit as part of their training programme.

There was another difference in riding Dick's horses in races: when I went to Ilsley he had one of the best stables in England. They were hand-picked horses. There was a lot of class, wherever you looked. I think every horse he had won a race that year. A lot of his horses were front-runners, though that was more me than him. When you're riding one of his, you know it's going to get you to the end. If it's the best horse in the race, making the running means that it's out of trouble and as long as it doesn't pull, but relaxes in front, there's no reason why a horse won't win. They're fit, so if you get to the front you never look back. Dick's approach as a trainer was a bit different from Bernard's. Bernard was more interested in what you had to say about a horse, while Dick was really more interested in how you went through a gallop than how you felt at the finish. Being a horseman himself, he was always interested in everything a horse did, right from the time you got on it, because it all means something.

At first I didn't take any notice of the Queen's Dunfermline. I was more interested in other horses like Relkino and Boldboy – mind you, I could hardly ride them because I couldn't hold the bloody things. Dunfermline had got beat before the Oaks. After I won the Oaks I went back to the yard, had a look at her and said, 'Which one's that?' I really hadn't been taking much notice of her at all and it was a bit of a shock to me that she won. She won easily, though it wasn't regarded as a very good race.

Just before that race I was driving down the little one-track road from Eastbury in my new Ferrari, which I'd bought through Suzanne Kane, who knew someone who imported them. There was an Austin 1100 coming the other way so I pulled in to the side but the other driver couldn't stop and he slid all along the side of my Ferrari. I got his name – it was Ben Wise and he lived in Eastbury – and then I was in a real panic. I had to get to the races but I couldn't drive the Ferrari there so I took it back to Eastbury and hopped into a brand new Golf GTI which had been delivered the day before and hadn't even been on a journey. By this time I was late and I sent a message to the course that I would miss the first race.

Of course Dick panicked and started looking round for jockeys for Dunfermline. Then I turned up in this other car. Mr Ben Wise was very lucky: I don't think he had any insurance. I can remember his wife in the car, screaming at him, and the kids in the back. Anyway, because I won the Oaks I didn't bother to get in touch with him but just paid for the damage myself.

After the win on Dunfermline I went upstairs with the Queen Mum, who was absolutely over the moon, beaming from ear to ear, and we spoke to Her Majesty on the phone, there and then, upstairs. She was so pleased she gave me a pair of cufflinks.

Relkino won the Benson and Hedges Gold Cup. He was one of those horses that wouldn't really settle in a race. He always pulled too hard and was a front runner because you couldn't hold him. One of the few times when I did hold him was at Epsom. I was behind Piggott and he came off the fence and my horse started running away with me and was going for the gap. I really couldn't stop it, he was such a big strong devil. Piggott saw me coming, and dived in on the rail. There was white paint flying everywhere. I thought it was a bit uncalled for and it's lucky he didn't ruin that horse's career. I think it was one of the reasons that the horse, Marinsky, turned savage.

Then Dunfermline won the Leger, beating Piggott on Alleged, the only time he was beaten. Alleged had won the Voltigeur by miles and Dunfermline had been beaten in the Yorkshire Oaks, when she was under a cloud – it turned out afterwards that she was coughing. We were very hopeful of winning the Leger. She was an out-and-out stayer, with a little bit of class, of course. I think Lester actually made a tactical error that day, he went too soon on Alleged. He led into the straight. I sat behind him and then came and beat him.

In my excitement getting past him I was a bit tough on the filly with the whip and she moved in a bit and there was an enquiry. But this was one of the few times that Lester didn't go for the jugular. He said, 'Don't worry, nothing happened.' He was fine. I suppose he must have seen me getting a bit uptight.

We thought we should perhaps have beaten Alleged again in the Arc but I got lulled into a false sense of security. I got myself in behind him, just behind the pace, and was boxed in. The pace became slower and slower and I couldn't do anything about it. The race was run too slowly for me. I don't know whether Lester rode it like that to beat me. I ran on to finish third and in all fairness you could say that we were unlucky. It was a good tactical race by Piggott, though, and made up for the bad one at Doncaster.

The championship was still in my mind. I still thought I had things to prove and things to learn but it was starting to come together and I was beginning to have real confidence in myself. I got confidence just from being attached to the Hern yard. I was sitting on Classic horses and doing the right things. And I had the confidence to go out and take chances.

In 1978 I was champion again. Ted Eley was still running things from Newmarket – I was very keen. I rode 986 horses, my busiest year. You don't think about becoming champion until halfway through the year. If things are going really great, you go for it. Even if they're not you still try to ride winners, but if you're going for the championship you put in that little bit of extra effort. Dick didn't like it. He was always at me, saying I was on the road too much. He used to worry that I'd burn myself out.

Troy was a two-year-old that year. We knew he was quite good, one of the better ones. He ran in the Royal Lodge, the race that taught me more about him than any other. I thought I had only one horse to beat, Lyphard's Wish. He was a front runner, so I decided to lie up with him then come and beat him at the finish. So I laid up with him and cut my own throat.

Troy died, never finished. Ela-Mana-Mou came from six or eight lengths behind to beat me. I decided then that that wasn't the way to ride him. He had to be given plenty of time to build up. You had to take your time with him early in the race.

I'd say that helped us to win the Derby with him because they went fast and I came into that turn miles behind. I actually thought that I wasn't going to win it. I was too far back coming round Tattenham Corner and it wasn't clever being that far back. I was just saying to myself, there's no point hustling him, be cool, if he doesn't win, he doesn't win, just be cool. I knew if I hustled him he wouldn't finish.

He won the King George – struggled a bit but won it confidently – then struggled in the Benson and Hedges when he went down in distance. Things were happening too quickly for him and I had to get at him before he was ready to run. He only won by three-quarters of a length. Then it was the Arc. The ground came up a bit dead and he was definitely a far better horse on firm. He just didn't quicken because of the ground. He had had a long season.

Troy was a big bloke but he was always an athlete. Everything about him was so easy. That horse never sweated. In the stalls at Epsom I turned to whoever was on my right and said, 'Look at his neck.' When you have given a horse a bit of exercise he gets a bit of powdery white on his neck. In the gates in the Derby he had that: powder, not sweat. He was never under pressure. He was a great athlete.

Dick would line his two-year-olds up in March/April time and try to work out which one would be a star. You can narrow it down. The two-year-olds are cantered up in bunches: two-furlong spurts. That's for education, teaching them how to go about it. And then once they have had lots of education they go three furlongs. And then they get to the stage where they start going down to the five. When they are really fit enough, before the ground becomes firm, Dick gallops them three furlongs flat out, in groups of four. That will be the last you see of the big, backward horses until they are more mature. He does all that in one day.

That surprised me terribly when I first saw it. I thought, 'What is this man doing?' But watching over the years I saw the sense in it. It's done for the horses, because they don't flop about as much afterwards. They get keyed up. Some horses' eyes are poking out of their heads for two weeks after, it really gees them up. It makes them point their toes, they're not all flabby and they get a hold of themselves. And although he puts them away, they're still doing two canters every day and perhaps a little bit of half-speed or fast canter. After they have had that, horses know themselves.

In the 1978 Derby I rode a horse called Admiral's Launch. He was a cracking horse, the best I'd ever ridden at that stage. There was so much excitement over him and although the confidence was waning because he'd been beaten – he'd let us down in the Guineas – I still thought he could win at Epsom. His gallops at home were unreal – just like Nashwan. He was murdering good horses. Then we got him on the racecourse and he fell apart. I imagine he must have been a bleeder.

I was knackered at the end of the season. I went to bed. You do find even now that when you stop riding it's like shutting the factory doors. You don't realise how tired you are. The adrenalin is still running when you get up in the mornings, but you've got very little to worry about, no excitement. You're low, you go downhill. You catch colds and flu. Always at the end of the year. If I'm going to get anything wrong with me, it's always then. You fight colds off during the season, just go through them. You don't feel good, of course, but you keep going: you've got adrenalin, things happening. The excitement means that it doesn't hurt as much.

I met Elaine that winter, Troy's year. I met her at a jocks' dinner. Mark Birch said there'd never been a champion jockey attend an annual jockeys' dinner and I said I would definitely come if I was champion and I did.

Because my relationship with Suzanne was starting to get a bit funny, I went on my own. George Cadwaldr had invited Elaine. He'd rung her up out of the blue. I was sitting next to her. I was staying at Doug Francis's the following evening to go to a charity dinner and I said, 'Would you like to come to the charity dinner?' She said, 'Yeah.' So I took her along and that's how it all started.

Things weren't going too well with Suzanne at the time. There was pressure on us to marry and I thought, no way. There were a few rows but it ended quite amicably.

Dick and Sheilah had found a cottage for me in Ilsley. They were very helpful. I think Sheilah found it quite draining but I hope she enjoyed doing some of it. She got carpets for a quid from a man called Mr Dunkley. She loved coming to me for money.

Elaine wasn't on the scene at that stage. She was there, in the background, but I wasn't really seeing her. At the end of Troy's year Suzanne and I had gone to Australia. That trip was the end of our relationship and we knew it. In fact I was surprised that she went; I suppose she was hanging on.

In 1980 I had my best year ever. I won everything: seven Group Ones including five Classics, and second in quite a few more. We had a very trouble-free sort of year, whereas Newmarket had a very poor year, struggling with coughing and the virus. That helped us.

The first Classic was on Known Fact in the 2,000 Guineas. I rode what I thought was a good race, did everything right, and got beaten by a better horse. And then after about five minutes I heard there was a problem with the winner, and I couldn't understand it. The enquiry had nothing to do with me at all. Nureyev's trainer was very upset when they threw the winner out and gave me the race. I was over the moon.

In June I won three Classics in five days. Henbit in the Derby on Wednesday, then Bireme in the Oaks on Saturday. Then on Sunday I went to France to ride Policeman in their Derby. Sheilah Hern had a party that day and was cross when I told her I couldn't go. She said I was missing it to ride a no-hoper. When I got to France, I had lunch with a few people in Paris. Pat Eddery and I left in different taxis for Chantilly – I got there okay but Pat's taxi driver took him to Longchamp by mistake. He had a fancied ride in the race and only just got there in time.

In the race itself I made the running. The others must have let me go, thinking, that's no bloody good, we'll catch it later, they were too busy worrying about each other. So I got away from them and they couldn't catch me. A friend of mine, Mike Oliver, had come over with me. He'd thought, I've come over with Willie, I'd better have a little bet on him. So he stood in the queue to have a bet, only when he got to the front it wasn't the tote. It was the ladies loo. He didn't get a bet on and he had to watch me win at more than 50–1.

12

CRASH AT YORK

It's a miracle it doesn't happen more often. Stand close to the rail, watch the horses thunder by and imagine a leg snapping in the midst of them. No warning, no time to aim for safety, just the ground coming up to smack you and a dozen sets of passing hooves likely to hammer you as they go.

At times Willie wasn't that keen on discussing or even fully acknowledging Silken Knot's fatal fall at York in August 1981. That's not surprising. If you are still practising a profession, it's hardly healthy to recreate the moments when it went shockingly, sickeningly wrong. But when he did talk, the memory was clear. It was as bad as it looked at the time.

I remember the ambulance. That day I was one of the television commentators. We saw the fall and winced at the replay. Anyone watching it was in heavy need of reassurance. It was my luck to be flannelling away to the camera when the ambulance came by. Inside it was Willie Carson and it was going the speed of a hearse.

Normally, once the stretcher is loaded, the ambulance speeds down the track and off to hospital faster than a healthy horse could gallop. Yet here was the one with Willie inside going by as if it was trying to hold together broken eggs. A horrible silence fell over the normally noisy stands. Jolly TV smiles were very much not the order of the day.

Perhaps there's another miracle. That the mind which still remembers doesn't cower at the thought of repetition. Go stand at the rails again. But don't think about it.   U

The fall at York in 1981 wasn't the worst I've had. It looks it but to me the worst one came later, in 1984 in Milan. I was riding a certainty – Apoldream, one of the best sprinters in Italy – and I was getting run away with. I had the race sewn up, it was just a case of not releasing him too soon. Then the horse in front of me just moved in and mine clicked into the heel of its rear leg. Apoldream went down and I was thrown up in the air, sky high. I remember coming down, hitting the ground which was as hard as concrete and breaking my ribs, my wrist and two fingers. I was hurting everywhere. I had no skin on my backside.

Elaine was watching the Wimbledon final on TV when the commentator suddenly said, 'By the way we've had a flash from Italy that Willie Carson has had a fall.' She started ringing all round Italy trying to find me.

When I got back to London the car was broken into. Elaine had brought all our gear. There was a briefcase with everything in it, addresses, cheque books, quite a lot of money. It was like losing our office.

I was off for five weeks because of that fall. It was the first season since 1970 I didn't ride a hundred winners.

The fall at York was from a filly called Silken Knot. Her form was in and out, not all that great. Dick didn't trust her so he put blinkers on her and we went into the Yorkshire Oaks quite confident that she'd win. But she was a bit reluctant to run, perhaps because she had this unforeseen problem. Suddenly her leg went snap. No reason, she just made a bad step and crash. She put her other leg out to save herself and it too went crack, so down we went.

That's all I remember until I woke up in the ambulance with Dr Allen. I've no idea how he got in there. I don't know where we were at the time but I remember hearing him say, 'Straight to hospital.' The next thing I knew I was lying in casualty. Elaine turned up. I was trying to be nice to her. I said, 'What the hell are you doing here?' and then burst into tears. That's the last I remember until I woke up next day in hospital. The Queen's surgeon was sent for, a neurologist from Leeds. He checked me over. I wasn't awake at the time and the only reason I know he came is because he sent me a big bill.

I wouldn't be riding again until the following year. I had a cracked skull, severe concussion, fractured spine, fractured left wrist. I was in good form in hospital but when I got out, oh dear. . . . Two weeks afterwards I was in a terrible state. I had headaches – I've had headaches ever since. I couldn't walk. I was well bashed around. I never saw my boots and breeches but apparently they were in a terrible condition. I became depressed. There was a time when I thought I might not ride again. I just kept getting worse and worse and worse. All I was doing was sleeping and sleeping. I had to be lifted out of the bath. I got to the stage where I virtually broke down.

Then I thought something was wrong because I couldn't feel any more pain. And that's the day I started to recover. I chucked all the pills away. They got me into such a state that I didn't take any more. And I began to feel better.

The foundations of our new house had been laid the week before York. We decided to slow it down. I became scared about the finances.

In the following January and February I started hunting. That was the beginning of my programme for coming back. Half a day at a time. I couldn't take any more. I was so weak I could hardly hold a horse. It was just a matter of mending my body back to normal strength. I had been drained, totally drained.

I had a headache for six months after the fall. It worried me but what could I do about it? I didn't tell the doctor. I don't complain about the headaches that much. But a lot of people told me that the accident changed me, my mentality. It changed my outlook on life. I wasn't so happy-go-lucky. Life had been great fun before, everything was a joke, riding was a joke. I'd been determined to be a jockey, determined to win and be clever in my job and I don't think anything ever worried me. Until the accident.

As well as hunting I did a bit of training so that I'd be fit for Doncaster. Then, three weeks before, Longboat chucked me off on the all-weather and chipped my flaming shoulder. On my first ride back I finished third. I suppose I had to show people that I could still ride so I rode the bloody thing the whole way. But I wasn't fit; mentally I was all right but physically I wasn't a hundred per cent ready. After the race I felt terrible. I had a burning sensation. My legs were jelly walking into the weighing room and my lungs were burning, on fire. I had to lie down. The next day I had a winner.

It took until Chester for me to be back as I wanted to be, though. It takes a long time to get really a hundred per cent physically well. I could hear the little grumbles in the background: he's gone, his nerves have gone. The desire to carry on increased after that.

My memory is not what it was since the accident. One morning I was supposed to be doing TV-am. They rang up and I was still in bed, and they said, 'Aren't you doing TV-am this morning?' It was so embarrassing.

There have been other injuries along the way, too. I can remember I was knocked senseless out hunting in the late sixties. My horse fell right on top of me. I broke two ribs and did some damage to my hips and ended up with a bit of arthritis.

Although my body still works the same now as when I was younger – it still has the same output, the same strength – it's just not as quick. I could still run to Middleham and back, I could still pedal a bike fourteen miles. I could do it, but not as quickly.

I remember puffing as I pulled up one day at Warwick and thinking I'd either got to stop riding or to stop smoking. That's when the smoking went.

I do find it hard to get fitter now. I'm somehow more aware of the winters. They've become shorter somewhere and there's less time to get fit. I'm a bit more careful with myself in the winter these days, I don't let myself go as much as I used to. I would get seven or ten pounds heavier at one time, but now I only put on three or four. Working on the stud involves a lot of heavy manual work. It's totally different from my London period. Now I'm in my wellies, digging, fencing or mucking out. I ride the hunters for exercise, too, which I never used to do. All these little things make me more active in my rest period. I also run from home to the bridge, three and a quarter miles. I start running three weeks before racing starts and gradually get quicker and quicker.

Elaine helped me a lot after the fall. We got married in 1983, on Cheshire Oaks day. It was a really exciting day for me, one of the happiest of my life. I simply enjoyed the whole day. When I got to Chester I was fined for not bringing my medical book. That's the Jockey Club to a tee – you go to your wedding and straight from the church to the racecourse, and they fine you for not bringing your medical book. Typical. You're hardly going to think about taking it to your wedding are you?

I got a letter about the OBE in August 1983. Great honour. It was at the time when Maggie Thatcher gave a lot of sporting people honours, and I was invited to a reception in Downing Street. It was very nice to be in the place and to have a look at the paintings. Talking to her I realised just what a determined lady she was. I tried to put up an argument but no way – it was something about racing needing more money, but oh, dear, off she went, there was no stopping her. She can talk.

Going to see the Queen was quite incredible. You are briefed on what to do: you have to go along, turn to her and walk forward, then go out. You can have one person with you and the audience sits and watches. There is a band playing. I spoke to the Queen about horses, I think I said 'we could have a Derby horse, ma'am. Church Parade.' At the time I thought he was a good horse. I was only allowed about fifteen seconds with her because she had so many other people to do. I couldn't believe how many people get honours. They were queueing up. She had to stand there giving out badges for four hours.

13
HERN'S ACCIDENT

It was the biggest test. A setback not to himself or his family. The hard little guy from Stirling had long learnt to live with that. But to someone central to his professional world. The crash that crippled Dick Hern.

As we have seen, Willie had had his own wounds in 1984, sidelined for so long by that fall in Milan that he failed to beat a hundred winners for the first time since 1970. But what happened in December was much, much worse. In many ways he had the best job in racing. In eight years with Dick Hern he had won ten Classics and three jockeys' championships. There would be more Classics, more big winners. But it didn't look like it in December. Nothing now could ever be the same again.

We had come a long way from the unpretentious scuffler who was keen to talk to anyone who bothered to ring. There were heavy responsibilities now. And they were not going to hang easy.   ℧

Dick's accident was the biggest incident in my life in a sense. That accident changed the course of umpteen lives, perhaps a hundred. Elaine and I had just come back from abroad when the phone rang. We were told that Brian Taylor had been killed. I felt drained. Then that same evening the phone went again. It was Sheilah Hern. She told me she had had a call to say Dick had been in a riding accident. She told us not to worry. He had been taken to Leicester hospital, then up to Stoke Mandeville. We went straight away to see him. He was not in good shape. He couldn't move anything. The only thing he could do was talk.

Yet his morale was fantastic. I remember going to see him one day and he said, 'I can move it.' 'You can move what?' I asked. 'My finger,' he said. He had those oddly-shaped hands people have when they've been paralysed. It was his thumb. I said, 'Let's have a look.' It moved just a fraction and that was what was exciting him. It didn't excite me. I'll never forget that. 'I can move it, look, I can move it,' he had said. He'd been in hospital for weeks by then. The progress was so slow.

I was never really worried about West Ilsley because Dick's mind was still concentrated on the place. I felt that he would point us in the right direction. I was half-confident that things would get back to normal. I started to take a bit more notice of what was going on on the training side. Marcus Tregoning, Dick's helper, was a brick. After Dick's accident they'd got him back from New Zealand and he went to the hospital every day and came back with the orders. Geordie, the head lad, looked after the horses in the evening. There were times when perhaps you would rather have done things a bit differently but you didn't know whether to say anything. I just went on merrily and did what I thought best. I didn't discuss things too much. It wasn't perfect but it worked reasonably well.

He came out of hospital in March. Far too soon. He was defying the doctors, doing a lot of office work. I thought everything was going smoothly. We had worked the horses quietly and had moved them from cantering into half-speed. Straight away he took charge. He came back, said, 'I'm in charge,' and that was it, even though he wasn't feeling well. The only thing that goes round in that man's head really is horses.

He kept improving slightly for eighteen months. He worked at it with great determination. You could see it was hard work but eventually he could walk with the aid of a frame. He tried different things to get around in, and an ordinary Shogun jeep worked as well as anything.

It was late spring, the Guineas meeting of '85, when I started believing we had a problem, that the horses had a cough or a virus. I wasn't happy with them. They weren't finishing. They had run reasonably well at first and should have come on, but they didn't. But Dick wasn't for listening. He wanted to prove that everything was still the same so he pushed on. I kept telling him we had a problem but he wouldn't accept it because he was too determined to prove himself. By the time June came he had to accept it and in fact he apologised to me.

There was nothing wrong with him wanting to prove himself, but it just so happened that the horses did have the virus. In normal years he would have taken a pull, we'd have had a quiet time with them and got over it. But he'd pushed and I think he knocked a few horses. When you get a virus and don't take a pull you don't get over it as quickly.

It was a very low point. The horses were running tailed off. Everyone was sick. My head was touching my boots. I can still remember some of the lads trying to buck me up, telling me not to worry, to keep going, keep trying. But they knew it was the horses.

Things were starting to go wrong and pressure was mounting up on Dick. I was always pretty free with the press, always telling the truth. I was talking about horses without consulting him and he was getting into a very embarrassing position because owners were finding out about their horses from watching TV or reading the papers. So I was told to shut up.

Then the press resented me for not being open and started writing things that were very harsh. Not always untrue, but hard. It annoyed me and I retaliated. I found it difficult but once you get into a groove it becomes easier.

Suddenly my whole world had gone. Dick Hern's stables were disintegrating, falling around our ears. And the press weren't on my side. They were very hard times. I was starting to doubt my own riding. There would be a bit of light at the end of the tunnel every now and again but it was the gloomiest period of my career. There was no fun in it any more. The laughing, the joking had gone. There was no buzz. Trying to ride winners was becoming serious, hard work. I don't think I was making mistakes. People say jockeys are riding well or badly but that's not the point. It's whether they're getting on the right horses or not. If you get on the right horses you make the right decisions and you win. John Dunlop went quiet at the same time. Losing his son in a car accident was a terrible blow to him. I had a mortgage on the house and stud so I had to keep earning. Things were going sour.

14
WEST ILSLEY CRISIS

Much unhappier things have happened since. The Royal Family has been beleaguered by such personal crises that you can bet they would willingly swap the lot of them to go through the Dick Hern affair again. But at the time the decision not to allow the wheelchair-bound Hern to continue his royal West Ilsley lease caused a stir unthinkable in a camp so centrally devoted to royal patronage. Up till then racing people were the last set of subscribers to the Divine Right of Kings. But now the Queen seemed in the wrong. Most horribly so.

It was an unhappy and in many ways an unfair saga. Don't doubt there were good intentions. But even courtly roads can lead to hell, especially when passions run high and the numbing cloak of royal secrecy throttles what might have been a much healthier debate.

It even got to hacks like me. Reporting in the *Sunday Times* on the crowd's fêting of Dick Hern after Nashwan's great 2,000 Guineas triumph at Newmarket, I told of how a senior Jockey Club figure had advised me to 'go for the jugular' in the column and I commented, with absolute accuracy, that 'feelings were running at an unprecedented height'. All too soon it was being put around royal circles that I was advising readers to 'go for the jugular'.

But Dick Hern had been very sick. It was an unhappy time. ⋃

By 1987 we were coming out of the woods. We had had the virus. People had lost confidence in us, some were leaving us, but we were just starting to click again. Of course we had won the King George VI with Petoski in '85 and the Gold Cup with Longboat in '86. But now we had Unfuwain and Minster Son as Classic-standard three-year-olds, with three good two-year-olds in Prince of Dance, Nashwan and Al Hareb. And then the heart attack came.

One day during that summer Bill Cook had looked at Dick Hern and said, 'That man won't be alive next year.' Dick did look terrible. You would be talking to him about the horses and he would be falling asleep.

Then at the end of July he had the heart attack. He'd been rushed into hospital once before and come out again. When it happened a second time he was virtually gone. But they opened him up and got him going. It was only a leaky valve but it must have been getting worse and worse, with the pressure of all the other things wrong with him. In a healthy body it would probably have worked better; in a seized-up one it must have been under tremendous pressure. And he had terrible asthma.

Alex Scott had been the assistant. He was going to start training the following year and was planning to go to the sales to start up his own stable. After the heart attack he offered to stay on and keep things going but Lord Carnarvon stepped into the breach and virtually took charge. For some reason he wanted somebody new to come in and look after the place. We all thought that William Hastings-Bass would turn up there and then, but he didn't. I don't suppose he could leave his stables in Newmarket.

The problems about Dick's future started when he had the heart attack. When he first went into hospital Carnarvon (then Lord Porchester) seemed to want to start being a trainer. He used to go over and look round the horses, keep the lads till seven at night. We were all getting a bit sick of it. It was said that he was taking over and it was creating a problem in the yard. Dick heard about it and said to Carnarvon, 'I don't want you to go to the yard.' I don't think that went down too well, being told to keep away.

Dick was still in hospital when he was told that he would have to leave West Ilsley. Sheilah was in a terrible state. She had two weeks to get out of the house. What does one do? Sheilah doesn't know whether her husband is going to live and she's told to get out of her house! Where does the poor woman turn? I don't know about Her Majesty buying bungalows, but you can't build a bungalow in two weeks. Sheilah was told to

ABOVE: Admiral's Launch was a cracking horse, the best I'd ever ridden at that stage. His gallops at home were unreal

LEFT: The best thing that happened to me in racing was winning the Oaks on Dunfermline for The Queen. I was always a royalist and always will be

BELOW: Being The Queen's jockey was a big thrill. Putting on those colours . . .

RIGHT: India was a big education for me. The racecourse was in the centre of Calcutta, surrounded by poverty. This is me after winning the Maneesh Memorial Cup in 1969

BELOW: I don't pretend to be a great brain but I enjoy all sports and it was fun meeting all the different people

BELOW RIGHT: Cassius put his hands in the air, rolled his eyes and said, 'Don't let's have any trouble now, little brother'

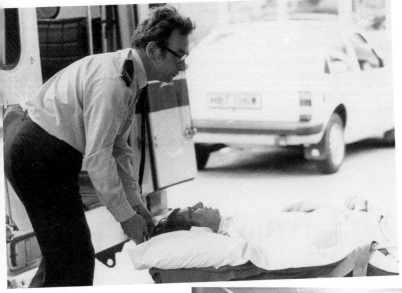

LEFT: Her leg just went snap and down she went. That's all I remember till I woke up in the ambulance

RIGHT: Elaine was a great help while I was recovering from the fall. We got married in 1983 and this is us the year after

ABOVE: Getting the OBE was a great honour, though I only had fifteen seconds with The Queen. She had to stand and give out badges for four hours

TOP: Lester made a tactical error in the Leger, he went too soon on Alleged. I sat in behind him in the straight then came and beat him

ABOVE: Troy was a big bloke but was always an athlete. Everything about him was so easy

LEFT: I got tired of holding Sun Princess, so coming down the hill I let her go. She won the Oaks as a maiden by twelve lengths

BELOW: I bred Minster Son myself so winning on him was something special

ABOVE: I have so much respect for Dick, I would jump off bridges for him

ABOVE: Nashwan was just very, very special

LEFT: I hadn't thought Salsabil would stay a mile and a half. Sheikh Hamdan insisted she run in the Oaks. This was a golden period for him

BELOW LEFT: Someone said that if an American jockey had ridden Dayjur he would have won. Which is quite true, because they'd have knocked the shit out of him. They might have fallen off as well

ABOVE LEFT: Flying is a great relaxation. I use the plane as much as I can and fly it myself with Bilko (Alan Biltcliffe). Mind you we have a modern Piper Saratoga not this Spitfire with me in my Biggles kit

ABOVE: Mum and dad watching their Billy. They were terribly supportive to me early on so it's really good that they have a cottage on the stud nowadays. Mind you I keep them working

ABOVE LEFT: Elaine and I looking at the wildfowl pond. We have quite a collection and I love messing about with them. A bit like with my grandfather's pigeons back in Stirling. Life goes full circle

ABOVE RIGHT: It's always nice to win the Stewards' Cup, but it gives it that little bit extra being 3,500 winners

get out because William Hastings-Bass was coming in two weeks' time.

I don't know at what stage she was told that Dick would make a recovery or what kind of recovery it would be. But I think I remember Dick accepting the decision because he was feeling so bad. Then, when he started to feel a bit better, he shook himself, grabbed the phone and started to fight. If he hadn't, he would have been ousted there and then, never to be seen again.

So Neil Graham was brought over from America to look at and run the place, which I thought was a very silly thing: somebody who hadn't been in Ilsley in his life before, didn't know how Dick worked. You might as well have had a man from Mars. Neil was a nice fellah, in fact I thought he did a good job under difficult circumstances. He was very diplomatic, handled the owners well. But I still don't think there was any need for it. I still think the place would have gone on all right with or without Alex Scott. It would have ticked on to the end of the season. It was all set up, except maybe for a few different plans for the two-year-olds.

We were very suspicious of Neil because we knew he was a Carnarvon man and that everything would be reported back to Carnarvon. One had to be careful what one said. But Neil did well, especially with Minster Son, who was special to me because we'd bred him at home at the Minster Stud, and Lady Beaverbrook had bought him as a yearling. He had to be trained in a funny way, he needed so long to recover after every race. We only had a couple of weeks to get him ready for the Leger so he was galloped a lot before the race and his eyes were popping out when he ran. He never relaxed because it was a rough race, but we got him there.

Dick's heart operation seemed to have worked and he was out of hospital by the end of the season. In the end they had had to give him the year's lease he was entitled to. After that, things went quiet. But it still hit me hard. This was the second time in five years that the end of my career had seemed imminent.

Despite what happened, I still think the Queen is a lovely person. I still admire her. I'm still a royalist. I love the Royal family and think they do a terrific job. They work very, very hard and do a great job for us abroad. But the Queen did make a mistake – we're all entitled to make mistakes. Lord Carnarvon is now getting the blame and he doesn't come out of this at all well. He comes out as a man with a very cold heart. Perhaps he advised the Queen wrongly. In my opinion it was terrible advice. But the Queen didn't have to take his advice. Where does the buck stop? At the top. So you have to say that the Queen made a mistake even though Carnarvon was possibly the instigator.

After our successes in 1990 it looks even more stupid. But people have pride and don't like backing down. Why should the richest woman in the world back down?

The Queen lost a lot of friends. Not many people thought it was a fair decision. Then again I'm only seeing one side of the argument. I don't know what the other side looks like though it seems pretty thin. I can't see the logic in not renewing the contract of a very successful business. It was a business that was thriving, not going downhill. You don't shut down a company in its prime.

Sheilah and Dick's attitude was one of bitterness. Sheilah just felt disbelief. She used to come to the club and break down in tears. All this happening at a time when she was completely distraught about Dick – plus the fact that life for them was three times harder because he was in a wheelchair. She went through absolute hell. When Nashwan won the Derby it was a very poignant day. Not so much for the horse, it was the being applauded. Sheilah said she saw young men and old men crying. It was a very, very moving day.

Of course it's none of my business what Carnarvon and the Queen do – they wouldn't have mentioned it to me and I would never have been involved in any decisions like that. I'm just a loser because I was Dick's jockey. Technically I was West Ilsley's jockey. I had ridden for the Queen for a couple of years but my association with Ian Balding didn't flourish and eventually stopped. Ian's a nice fellah but he's a hard man to please and likes to change jockeys after two or three years. After that I wasn't the Queen's jockey any more.

The question of my being at West Ilsley the following year was never put to me. I wasn't consulted about anything. I took the view that they had made a wrong decision which was going to affect my career so I felt slightly bitter, slightly betrayed. I was part of the team, so indirectly I was being dismissed as well, which I think was very unfair.

Lord Carnarvon has never mentioned the move since. Nothing. I'm only a servant. I'm a paid employee, that's all.

15
NASHWAN

1989 could never be just another spring. While it hadn't yet been made public, the time-bomb of Dick Hern's royal lease was bound to explode. A Classic winner could be the only compensation, but from where would it come ?

The blooming of the Classic colt at the start of his three-year-old season is one of racing's most exciting natural phenomena. By the end of the two-year-old campaign a team like Dick Hern's would be well aware that they housed a performer of real potential. But neither they nor the pack of speculating press pundits can know how much improvement the winter will bring.

The break is such a long one for so young a runner. Usually October to April, five full months off the racetrack, almost half a year of development away from the public eye. And by the time they reappear, the colts are usually within two to three weeks of the 2,000 Guineas, which may be the race of their lives. They may even, as Dick Hern did with Brigadier Gerard and this time with Nashwan, go to the 2,000 Guineas without a previous run. Little wonder that reports of what happened on the gallops can make the fever rise.

Close-to it can be contagious. Up these gallops the champions have come. Could that be another Troy or Henbit that went thundering by? The whole idea of the Classic preparation is to build belief into the body and brain of the Classic colt. If he keeps passing those tests the belief passes into conviction amongst his following. No big-fight contender ever had a corner-man more committed than a stable lad whose horse has won a gallop of a morning. 'On my life I promise you,' will come the refrain as the drink is accepted at lunch-time, 'this could be a star. I was absolutely cantering over the others.' Buy him another and he will pledge you the heavens next.

With a Dick Hern colt reports rather than sightings were the most that we usually got. No easy public access like Newmarket or Lambourn. So if a new name was beginning to burn up those demanding downland gallops at West Ilsley, it would be the jungle drums that bore the message. In 1990, the rumble grew to a roar.

A star had come just when it was wanted. The arrival of Nashwan in any year would have been fantastic. His emergence that spring was little short of sublime. But he wasn't exactly as expected. ♘

Prince of Dance was the animal all the hopes were pinned on. He had really excited me as a two-year-old. He looked like a Triple Crown horse. He was a very brave horse because it turned out that he had a trapped spinal cord. It was Dick who noticed that he wasn't right when he watched a video of the horse in hospital and saw he was carrying his tail on one side.

I didn't think he'd been right in the Dewhurst. He hadn't worked as well before and I thought he was just starting to go. There was a big row after we'd dead-heated with Scenic in the race. Lord Weinstock asked me to object. Watching the film, there were grounds for demoting Scenic to second because there was interference, but I felt my horse had contributed to it by moving in, so I refused. Old Weinstock didn't go racing a lot. I used to have two-hour phone conversations with him once a week. But he didn't speak to me for two years after that. He was very upset and corresponded with Dick about it. He couldn't see why his horse shouldn't have got the race and he blamed me. Not that it made any difference to the future – I was in his bad books but I was still going out there doing the business for him. It didn't matter to me, I just laughed about it.

Anyway, I thought that he'd be a lot better the following year: the normal improvement, the extra distance. This horse is going to be special, I told myself. I had visions of him being the best horse I'd ever ridden. It was when he went lame on us that Nashwan came in. Nashwan was a good horse but I didn't have him built up as anything special as a two-year-old.

He had a big splint on his near-fore around February time, so he missed all the preparatory cantering and all the early galloping and he was behind all the other horses. He was still doing slow work while all the others were doing strong stuff and he was still hard on the bit. I had heard one of the work riders talking to the Guv'nor and it must have been exciting him because he was going up last, doing this fast canter and just letting him come up the side. Nashwan was really tugging. I saw him a couple of times. I'd go up first and he would go up last, and I could see that he was going really well, though not fast.

Then I had a ride on him. Oh, bloody hell, I said to myself, bloody hell this horse is going well. Great, big, lanky horse. Fantastic. The movement on him felt really lovely. I wanted to have a crack at him, but Dick told me I couldn't, not yet. Then it became clear that Prince of Dance wasn't going to make it and on the day of the Greenham I went along the trial ground with Nashwan.

It was the most fantastic piece of work. He beat them by a hundred yards. I'd been following the two others and I let him go in the last two furlongs. You could feel it. It was magic and when I looked round the others were out of sight. I said, 'What happened to you two?' I knew it was good work, but I had to have it confirmed. 'Why didn't you come with me?' They said, 'We couldn't.' Dick said, 'That's the best work I've seen since Brigadier Gerard.' I said to him, 'You're in the prime seat. All those lads in the distance there, they haven't got that much further to go, they'll all be down in Ilsley and all the phones will be busy. You've got a phone right there. I'd get on right now if I were you.' He didn't though. And when we went down through the village in the Shogun there were all the lads going off to breakfast, pedalling on their bikes. Everyone was rushing around that breakfast time. Not a lot of talk going on but everybody rushing around. Nashwan was 33-1 and he wasn't even a runner at the time. All the lads started getting on and the price started dropping and of course everybody started asking about the horse. I said, 'Yeah, he'll win.'

The second time I rode him he really confirmed it. Same result, same excitement. And he didn't blow much. The more I saw of him, the more confident I became. Nash the Dash: on 2,000 Guineas day the horse was invincible in my eyes. He was just very, very special. The last words the Major said to me were, 'Don't forget to let him use his stride.' The race went like Piaget clockwork. That year Guy Harwood seemed to be working for us. Every time we needed a pacemaker he gave us one. When we wanted a slow pace he sat behind us. It was uncanny. In the Guineas this horse of Harwood's jumped off and I was able just to sit on his heels. Funnily enough I was disappointed in a sense that Nashwan didn't win by further. But you have to remember that he hadn't had a preparation for this race. It was rushed on to him.

Coming back in I remember jumping off the horse and Maktoum Al Maktoum leaping back in fear. It was special. The horse hadn't had a previous race that season, there was all the publicity about us getting sacked and we had said, 'Up yours, we can still do it.'

All sorts of emotions flowed through me. All my friends said, 'This horse is 3-1 for the Derby.' I said, 'Take it. Back it now.' The whole of England was on the horse. I'd never been so confident of winning a race as I was winning that 2,000 Guineas. Whether I'd just hyped myself up I don't know, but twice a week I got myself hyped up because I went and sat on him and he just went whoosh.

Before the Derby everybody was pretty quiet up to the day of the race. The stable was just not in form, though Nashwan was. Two weeks before the Derby Dick likes to work them over a mile and a half, but it's an easy mile and half. They just canter through half of it. That was his way of doing things but I don't recall Nashwan working over a mile and a half. It was always in the back of my mind that he wouldn't get the trip but in the race I rode him on the assumption that he *would* stay. I always do. The hype was as big as the Guineas but then there was a lot of talk about Cacoethes, too. Talk of fantastic gallops.

I moved early. My sole intention was to keep my eye on Cacoethes, but in fact I got him too early. I rode on his tail and then I found myself going past. I always say that if you're going to attack a horse, do it and kill him off. You can sit on a lot of horses who cover a lot of ground but their stroke rate may not be that great. But Nashwan could power himself forward. It was as if he had six-inch nails in his feet and was grabbing the ground. That's the sign of a good horse. They're also well balanced, as Nashwan was. Lungs, ability, stride, temperament. Nashwan's flaw, if he ever had one, was his temperament.

I blame myself for what happened in the Eclipse Stakes. I panicked. I gave him a harder race than he need have had. Opening Verse got ten lengths clear and we all sat there and watched him. It was a hell of a race. Indian Skimmer, Warning, they were very good horses. And Opening Verse was given a very good ride. Two and a half furlongs out I thought I'd better go and get him and I did within a furlong. But of course I'd used up petrol. Nashwan was very tired. And the King George was two weeks later. The truth is that we shouldn't have run him in the King George. He was out, he needed a rest. This time we went a steady pace and Cacoethes quickened up better than me. But we got away with it by a neck. He was a very tired winner that day. He'd done a little bit of work the Saturday after the Eclipse but it wasn't that good. On the Tuesday he went out again and I said I thought we'd get away with it. It was then that we'd hatched the plan to go steady and just get away with it by using our superior speed. It worked, but only just.

Richard Hills was criticised by the Press for going too slowly on the pacemaker but that was the whole idea. If you look at the fractional times of the King George, the last six furlongs would have broken the track record at Ascot. Sprinters would have had trouble staying with us.

Before we went to France for the Prix Niel there was no sign of anything being wrong. Perhaps we weren't able to give him a long enough holiday. I think the horse got a bit stale, but having said that, in France he was trying to give seven pounds to two animals who came out and won Grade One races afterwards.

Also the horse wouldn't relax. He box walked. He wouldn't relax before the Eclipse either. He'd arrived at Ascot for the King George an hour before the race, so we knew there was going to be a problem going to Longchamp. I think he was blindfolded all night to keep him quiet.

Turning into the straight I was sitting reasonably quiet but Pat Eddery, on French Glory, said he could hear my horse choking, which I couldn't hear. Pat thought then that he had a chance of beating us. I was genuinely and sincerely shocked by the result. There was no indication from his work at home that he wouldn't win. His work was good. So I was shocked by the result. But then I hadn't heard about the troubles of the night before.

After that the Champion Stakes was the only race really in Sheikh Hamdan's mind. The horse came back, we kept him in work, but he didn't entirely please us. It was too chancy. He wasn't a hundred per cent, he'd had a long year and he hadn't got over his exertions in France. The decision was taken. He wouldn't run again.

16

SHEIKH HAMDAN

At the time most of us thought the words were the exaggeration of conflict. Willie spoke loud and loyal on Dick Hern's behalf but he also said 'I may have to retire.' He had been around so successfully and for so long that no one believed him. But in hindsight he would have been in trouble without a new patron. Without a magic carpet from the east.

Willie had been on the roller-coaster long enough to be cured of surprises, but even he cannot have guessed quite what a take-off point the West Ilsley crisis might prove to be. Far from being ground into extinction, the Carson career was to go soaring again with five more Classics and twenty-one Group Ones, and all because of the blue-and-white silks of Nashwan's owner Sheikh Hamdan al Maktoum.

The ruling family of Dubai has become so much part of the English racing scene that its input is almost taken for granted. It's no bad thing to take stock occasionally and gulp at the enormity of their support, the greatest investment in racehorses that the world has ever seen. Sheikh Mohammed may still be the leader in numbers and money won, some 185 winners and almost £2 million in 1992, but Sheikh Hamdan is never far behind. That same season saw 103 victories and over £1.1 million in money won.

Retirement will come. But these last years have tapped the richest source of the whole story. Not bad for someone who thought he had reached the 'Exit' door. ♘

The Carnarvon business went to the back of my mind because of Nashwan, though it was always there, niggling away. At the York spring meeting in 1989 it was announced that Dick could stay on at West Ilsley until the end of the year, which was a big help. God knows what he would have done if he had had to get out before. He didn't know where he was going. Nowadays there are yards galore on the market, but at that time there weren't. We were looking around for small yards for him. We were in a corner and it was a bit hectic.

I'm not as bitter as I was though it's a shame that I won't be riding the gallops in Ilsley again. I know them so well – Dick knows them even better. Yet there we were, in the twilight of our careers, setting out on a new venture. It's the sort of thing people do when they are twenty-eight. He was nearly seventy and I was nearly fifty and we were off to new ground (at Kingwood House Stables, in Lambourn, as it turned out).

It was getting late in the season and I hadn't got a job for the following year. Dick had cut down. The retainer would have to be reduced. Nobody would want to pay. What was I going to do? Sheikh Hamdan had offered to help, before Dick got the extension. So I got hold of his racing manager, Angus Gold, and said, 'Look, would you be interested?' I took what was offered. It was nothing very big, but I took it and I don't have any regrets.

Khalid Abdullah wanted to send Dick four horses which Pat Eddery would be riding. Dick asked me if he could have them. He wanted them because they would be four nice horses but I said no. It would set a precedent that I didn't want set. I said I didn't like having horses in the yard that I couldn't ride. He was loyal to me so I had to be loyal to him. I have so much respect for Dick, I'd jump off bridges for him.

I'm lucky to have had Sheikh Hamdan. Dick had started to struggle a bit with boxes and not enough horses. Sheikh Hamdan had come along later than Sheikhs Mohammed and Ahmed. We'd had a lot of expensive horses for them but hadn't found a good one. Then Hamdan came in and home bred from Height of Fashion, a mare he bought from the Queen.

Angus is supposed to be my guv'nor, though he doesn't behave like a boss. I talk to him, tell him everything. I only speak to Hamdan when there are things that he wants to know about – when he can't get hold of anybody else he rings me. Things like how a horse gallops, things that worry him. He doesn't ring up after a win, it's after gallops more than anything. He wants to know about the top horses. I see him occasionally in England but more usually abroad. The only time I saw him during 1990 was in France.

He seems to be an easy man to ride for. But he watches movies of every race – *every* race. What's my jockey doing, why did my jockey do that? He rides races all the time, is into the technical aspect. He'll say, 'I want you to go from the turn.' 'Yes, sir.' So I sit there to the furlong marker. And he'll say, 'Why don't you do as I say?' I just laugh. I do my own thing, but if I've got doubts I'll do it his way. Like Salsabil at Newbury. 'Don't wait,' he said, 'go, go, go.' He says I never do as he tells me. He's always telling me to go post quietly. And I say, 'Yes sir, I will do sir, yes sir.'

It all works pretty well. We're a good team.

Some people say the Maktoums have too many horses, but you only think that when you see them owning three-quarters of the runners in a maiden race. You don't say it when you're selling your horses to them at the sales. I think we're very fortunate to have them. It's also lucky that the brothers are competitive between themselves.

I went across to Dubai for the opening of the racing operation over there. They're going to get some good horses and it'll be another country with good racing. It'll never be the same as Europe because of the climate – there's only six months of the year they can race in because it gets too hot. I suppose there might come a day when they have an indoor, air-conditioned racecourse. It may well become a place where a lot of Europeans will go in the winter, because it's a real holiday place now with lots of facilities for sporting people.

17
1990

After Nashwan there should, by logic, have been anti-climax. Instead we got *annus mirabilis*. A jockey who thought he might be headed for the scrap heap was back aboard the best and the fastest. 1980 was a great year. 1990 nearly matched it.

English statistical tables rank jockeys only in number of races won, yet trainers are listed in the amount of money earned. By that latter token Willie was champion three consecutive years, 1989–91. In America they call it 'Stakes' earnings. In any language this was success. There were some fast horses for our man to steer. ♘

When I rode Dayjur in work at home I said, 'This horse is fast, he's never going to stay seven furlongs.' But Dick wouldn't have it. He had the horse mapped out for the Free Handicap and unfortunately I went into the race thinking I had to reserve his tremendous speed. I'd have been better off going flat out on him.

He'd been working superbly at home before his next race, at Newbury. I kept telling Dick he had speed to burn. He was going over six furlongs at Newbury and the ground was just a bit too easy. I was sitting there and sitting there, confident because I knew how he worked at home: when you went click, he simply took off. Then another horse came up beside me and I thought, I don't mind if you get half a length, I'll blaze you in a second. I was worrying about the trip because I knew my horse was not certain to stay. I held him and of course when I went click nothing happened. I just went up and down on the same spot and got beaten a head.

I remember Guy Harwood saying, 'You're a lazy jockey, you fell asleep there.' I jumped down and said, 'You bloody well train your own fucking horse.' I hadn't fallen asleep. It might have looked that way but I hadn't. I was confused by the horse. He was so brilliant at home. Anyway, we had a post mortem after that. I blamed the ground. He had won at Nottingham before Newbury when I think I'd let him run a little bit. That's when we came to the conclusion that we'd better go down to five. So we went to five at Sandown, then at Ascot. And that was the answer: just let the horse do his thing – run. I thought he was at his most spectacular in the Nunthorpe at York.

I'd made up my mind that I was going for it all the way. Everything was perfect. The going was perfect. The weather was perfect. And it all went brilliantly. I'd begun to believe beforehand that he was the fastest horse in the world and that day at York he really proved it to me. Towards the end of the race I could hardly believe it.

Dayjur was a quiet, amenable horse to ride. He wasn't a great big powerful horse. He didn't talk to me. He just went about his business and got the job done. You could see him concentrating. He'd get edgy and give me a bit of trouble in the stalls, so he had to go in late. He was just winding himself up, that little coil was getting all sprung up, and when the gates opened, whoom! Two strides it always took before he really started grabbing the ground.

The day before the Breeders' Cup I was having lunch with a group of Americans. 'You ever heard the name Day-gerr?' I asked them in my best American accent. 'Nope,' they said. 'Well,' I said, 'you will tomorrow.'

In the Breeders' Cup my biggest worry was the gate, because I knew the American horses were so much more revved up than ours. They have more practice and are into it much quicker. The jockeys beat the hell out of them, whack them to get them into top gear straight away. I knew that would be my biggest problem. I actually thought the high draw would be a help, but in hindsight it would have been better if we'd been drawn lower.

I honestly think Dick got a bit carried away with the horse. He was getting bigger and stronger and better and Dick had started to work him harder but really he only needed to be kept ticking over. We were all against it. The horse got himself in a state, though I tried to be as quiet as I could with him. That's when everyone saw him at Longchamp and said, 'This horse has gone.' He didn't like it much. He was a little horse, happy when he was doing things he knew about but worried by a change in routine.

I was in charge of the horse in Belmont Park for the Breeders' Cup. Dick still doesn't know what he did on the Friday morning. I went in the gate and thought it would be better if I didn't jump him because the more relaxed the horse, the quicker he jumps. So he stood in the stalls and came out backwards. Then I went a couple of furlongs with him and that was all he did.

He didn't get left in the race but he did drop behind in the first couple of strides. (Everybody thought he was a lightning-fast starter because he used to leave them behind after half a furlong, but his first two or three strides were not his fastest.) Then I laid down on him. I thought I had burnt him up to get there but when I got there I thought, okay, we'll ride the race now. One of our fellahs said that if an American jockey had ridden it he would have won. Which is quite true, because they'd have knocked the shit out of him. They might have fallen off as well.

That last furlong was terrible. At first I didn't know what he was doing. He pulled up dead. He was looking. He started off looking at the boards. You can hardly see it on film, but there are two boards along the rail and the sun had cast a square shadow on the grass. He hopped over it. And then there were all the other shadows underneath the rails at the winning post. Incredible.

I'd given him a crack and you'd think he would have been looking at the stick but as my hand came back to the rein I was up in the air. If he'd put his head down and raced again we might not have got back again before the end but there was still a bit in the tank. But he didn't. He popped the next shadow and landed awkwardly. There was nothing I could have done. Only a noseband would have stopped him seeing the shadows. Because they have eyes in the sides of their heads, horses can see backwards, forwards and down. With a noseband they can't see down, they can only see the ground ten yards in front of them when a shadow doesn't seem so black and white. He jumped the shadows because he's clever. He thought, 'There's something not right, I'm not putting my foot down there.'

All his career he had been either running up the centre of a track or racing on a dull day. Longchamp was the first time he had ever seen a shadow. It was a bit late in a horse's career to discover his fear of them.

Then of course there was Salsabil. I remember the first time she ever ran, at Nottingham over six furlongs. They'd told me they were hoping she was a bit special. She won brilliantly. I said to her lad when I came back in, 'You've got a Group One horse here.' I did get beat on her at two, when she was coming back from a lay-off and the ground was on the firm side. I should have let her run but I held her, I wanted to win but not to give her a hard race. She didn't find as much as I'd hoped and the other filly had too much for us. She must have been protecting herself on the ground.

As a three-year-old she kept on doing it. She had a lovely, well-oiled action, she'd pass horses without me pushing her, like she'd been kicked up the backside.

After the Guineas, I was one of the ones who thought she wouldn't get the mile and a half, and I was worried about running her in the Oaks. Then Hamdan stepped in and took charge of everything. This was a real golden period for him.

She was an exceptional filly.

18

RACE-RIDING

It's always special when a master craftsman talks about his trade. You can imagine the barrel, the glass, the chair being put together. When it's a jockey the image is even more vivid. You remember him atop the horse.

So many horses down the years that as you listen, you find the saddle rather than the wicker furniture of the Carson conservatory, to be his element. It seems almost strange to see him sitting here as a mere two-legged earthling. What you get with Carson, Eddery, and the Piggotts of this world is man as centaur. The universe they talk best of is bounded by the clanging open of the starting gates and ended by the final moment when the winning post flashes past.

Less than 100 lbs of man aboard 1,000 lbs of horse. So few of us have ever done it that discussion can be as distant as that of the mystic mountaineer. Not with Willie. He always talked his corner but now he speaks with the authority of the years. Fools aren't suffered too gladly and young jockeys can smart from the lash of the senior's tongue. But here's a man who has done it and is not afraid to say why.

It's been quite a while since Marija finished last that first day at Redcar. And the pilot's improved a bit too.   ∪

Over the years the standard of race riding has become much much better. Today's jockeys are more accomplished than they used to be. People don't panic like they used to. They accept things now. If you're boxed in, you're boxed in. If you move you'll only cause a problem, so you just sit there and funnily enough nine times out of ten something moves out of your way and you can go.

I don't agree with the whip rule as it stands, but I do agree that we needed some tighter regulations on the use of the stick.

Jockeys are better because of it. They're thinking a little bit more and some have had to alter their style. It hasn't been easy for some of the older ones but the young ones are going to benefit. I think the young jockeys that are coming along are going to be a lot better. They're going to learn quicker than people like me.

I was one of the lucky ones, though, because I've never been a stick-using jockey. I use two hands on the reins rather than one. That's my style and it fits well with the new whip ruling. That said, the specifics of the rule are wrong: the emphasis on numbers of strokes. There are old dears in Bournemouth counting off the TV and that's wrong. They should take the whole picture of the race and the temperament of the horse into account. Was the horse sticking his head out when he was being hit? Was he improving? Was he swinging his tail? These are all things that matter. If the jock keeps banging away and the horse isn't going forward then he *should* be punished because he shouldn't have persisted in hitting the horse. But if the horse was sticking his head out and trying, where has he gone wrong? There are times when you can hit a horse six times and hit it twice too often and other times when you hit a horse fifty times and it isn't enough. There are horses that won't even come out of the box unless you give them a   dig in the ribs. I'd like to get the rule changed so that the restriction on the number of strokes is knocked out.

The type of whip used is important, too. In America you could use a golf club if you wanted to, whereas South Africa has very strict rules about the size of the whip's flap, which has to be quite big. Germany has a rule that for two-year-olds sticks can only be twelve inches long. So the jocks put a big heavy flap on it and if you hit a horse with that it leaves a mark – it's worse than a whip. I nearly fell off when I tried to hit round the back with one. It's all a question of balance. I haven't been to Scandinavia for years, but they are the strictest of all on the whip.

You're still allowed quite a long whip here, twenty-two inches, which I would say is a sensible length. In America some of the riders use whips that are twenty-eight inches long. They look as if they're going fishing. I wouldn't say that helps a horse to run faster. The jockeys there are quite good with the whip, though, because they pick it up and change over the top quickly. People are experimenting with that over here now. I've tried it and I get in a tangle, but it's coming. I think in a few years it will be done that way.

Some people say whips are cruel. But why does a racehorse run fast? Because it's frightened. Racehorses are bred to be athletes but not all of them are. Some of them who are racing don't want to run fast. Not all kids are intelligent: they shouldn't go to university if they haven't got a brain, yet they're pushed there. It's the same with racehorses. They're bred to be brilliant but not all of them are. Some don't want to go, so they're bullied in training, pushed to go faster. Some of them are a bit laid back and if you just sat on them when you jump off on a gallop they wouldn't go fast, they'd just go up there in their own time. That's when you have to use the stick. It's fear. If you didn't have that stick they wouldn't be frightened of you. So a stick is the most important thing. It would be all right if we were all riding champions all the time. Then we wouldn't need a stick. But we're not. Ninety per cent of the time racehorses have to run through fear.

Some top horses are lazy, too. With them the stick is like a gear stick: you tap a horse down the neck and the thing will leg it. Just tap him down the neck and that leg goes out two inches longer. The stick is very important. When you get into a driving finish you hit behind the saddle to try to make the horse stretch, to get lower to the ground, to make that front leg go out further. You can't get a horse lower to the ground by pushing him. It's when you go 'whack, whack' that he pushes his front leg out further and gets more speed.

I suppose I am occasionally cruel on a horse but I don't look at it that way. If we had no whips we would have a poor quality of racing. What would happen is that those lazy horses would be bullied more at home, probably to the point of cruelty. I don't think things are too bad at home at the moment. I suppose there are people who are a bit cruel, but it's not all that bad. Without whips it would become worse. In the past, methods of training were much harder. People used to have ball bearings in a small box. Horses were trained at home to associate the rattling noise with being hit, with pain. And I believe that the Americans had a system whereby you had a battery and a buzzer and you would buzz at the same time as you gave the horse an electric shock. Then all you'd have in the race was the buzzer, and it worked by noise association.

I remember sitting on the gate at Brighton not so long ago and looking across at this Australian jockey. I could see blood seeping out of his horse's neck. I tackled him, and said, 'What the hell are you doing?' I threatened to report him. He disappeared. I think he had a pin and he pricked that horse. I still don't know to this day what he was up to. The horse was all right but I was shocked. It upset me.

Racing used to be a lot rougher than it is now. At one time riding at the age of forty-eight would have been a no-no. I think your nerve would have gone. That's possibly why jockeys didn't last as long. Before cameras were introduced, Lester Piggott was ruthless. He would have you hanging over the rail. He did it on purpose. It sounds terrible now, but several years ago it wasn't such a bad thing. It was a rough game and you had to look after yourself. You knew you had enemies, who were going to be after you. You didn't know who your friends were. I suppose money talked. That doesn't happen now, or if it does I should think it only happens up north. But it's not like it was. In my eyes racing is ninety-nine per cent clean.

In Australia it's the opposite to England: you're had in if you *don't* use the whip. They think you're not trying. There's a lot of noise in their races when all the whips crack. I've never noticed when I've been in a race, it's only when you stand down close by the rail that you hear it. No wonder the horses get frightened, with the cracking of the whip and the thunder of their heels, horses hitting their own feet, the rush of wind, the flapping of cloths. You can virtually hear muscles tear.

Here we do it a little bit more slowly and gracefully. We wind up into it. When you're riding a race in Europe, once everything has settled you virtually don't hear a sound. I suppose there is noise but you're blocking it out, concentrating. If you click heels with the horse in front it's like a gun going off.

I'm not saying the Australian system's wrong. I don't like it because I haven't been brought up with it. But I really don't think it makes sense, running so tightly bunched. Horses interfere with one another, become unbalanced. Flailing the whips is not very nice to look at, either, though I don't think it interferes with the horse as long as you're in rhythm. I wouldn't try to whirl my whip the Australian way. It's awful. It's just to increase the fear and to show the punter that they're trying. The punting down there is gigantic.

I find it very difficult riding in France. They always go too flaming slow there. I feel as though I want to go on but I'm always having to tell myself not to make a move before the last turn. You just don't: in France a race is never won until the line. The French were very, very strict about contact at one time, too. I remember riding Parnell in the Prix du Cadran and I slightly brushed another horse and lost the race. We should never have lost it but as their rules stood at that time, if you even touched another horse that was it. You need a straight line from the time you set off because if you get interfered with you're not going to win. And the horses fan out in the straight because they're sprinting then.

Some of the younger French jockeys ride incredibly short and I can see the sense in it, though they might change after they learn what suits them best. Everybody is different. I wouldn't criticise people about how they ride. It all depends on their own physical attributes. There's no one way that's right. It is important, though, to keep a tight hold of the horse's head. The tighter you hold them, the more frightened of you they are, the faster they will go. When you've got them slack they're not frightened.

When I ride I don't have much to eat first. Just something light and a glass of white wine – but not too much. I remember once being held up getting back from Oslo with Eric Eldin. One of the jumps boys had had a winner and while we were waiting the champagne began to flow. It was Monday morning and we were riding at Alexandra Park that evening. The start of one race was just in front of the stands. And poor Eric fell off. Jockeys don't drink as much these days. Everything is much more professional. There are better diets – in the old days, a diet meant doing without.

Of today's jockeys, Pat Eddery would be my best mate. Pat is a very determined fellah and a very effective rider. His memory for races is phenomenal. He's a hard man to beat. As with all jocks, when you get out on the course we're rivals but that's not the same in the weighing room afterwards.

I find that I'm actually closer to my hunters than I am to racehorses. I don't look after racehorses so I don't get attached to them the way the lads do. I only get attached to them because of their ability, because of what they do for me. I don't get to know their characters as intimately, though there are some, such as Gallant Hope and Creeager, that I've become fond of.

Although the standard of riding has gone up, the standard of stewarding has gone down. In the old days the stewards just didn't take much notice. You'd ride a horse that wasn't doing its best and instead of being hauled in for a big enquiry, you'd just saunter in after the race and wherever you were, old Roscoe Harvey would come and sit beside you. 'Willie, that horse, would I be right in backing it next time?' he'd say, or something similar. 'Well, I don't think you'd be far wrong in doing so.' And that would be a bollocking: he was telling you that he'd noticed and you knew that if you went out on that horse again, he'd be watching. He was the head one but they were all a bit that way inclined. They weren't there to do you, not like today. All they want to do now is to get you in front of the stewards and have an enquiry.

Things could be improved if there were better camera angles, and better eyes watching racing – more educated eyes – though you'd have to pay for them. America is run totally by ex-jockeys and they can be the hardest men to ride for. They've been through it themselves and know what is interference and what isn't, what is accidental and what isn't.

In this country, if the stipendiary stewards have got their knife into somebody, they make sure that person gets done. The stipe puts over the evidence and points out the rules, lays down the law to the stewards. The stewards don't always take notice, but it's the stipe who brings things to their attention. I don't have confidence in ex-army officers who've had no experience of riding a horse. Failed army officers, I should say, because if they weren't failures, they wouldn't be doing this job.

It's not just the stipes that are bad, though, it's the whole system. They should get away from this ex-army officer system. It's just because they can speak, and say 'sir', and that's not the answer. Unfortunately the ex-jockey would not have had the education of an ex-army officer. He wouldn't be able to portray a story, he wouldn't be articulate enough.

In America they sit in a nice air-conditioned box at the top of the stand with a lot of equipment in front of them. They can just hit a button and get an instant re-run. By the time the jockey gets back, they either get on the phone to him by the scales or, if the jockey wants to protest, he grabs the phone and rings them. By the time the jocks get back to the weighing room, the enquiry is virtually over.

I don't know what system I want exactly, I just know that ours is not right. If the stipendiaries were better people you could give them a vote. They often have their knives into me, because I answer them back. I say what I think, tell them they're bloody idiots. Always have done. I've near enough been suspended for that alone.

Stewards are supposed not to bet, either, but they do. They're worse than jocks. It's human nature. And if they're betting when they're stewarding, they're bound to be biased. All you have to do is go to the stand and watch to see who bets down the rails. A steward who'd had a bet wouldn't be able to turn a black and white case, but if it's fifty-fifty, you know at once which way it's going to go. They always give you a fair hearing whenever you go in, and you can put your case over, but sometimes it's just not worth bothering. Stewards do get things wrong.

19

FAMILY

It's the cosiest place. Willie Carson's den, the trophy-filled sitting-room off the far corner of the hall, is a temple to his talent. Within its four walls, with their neatly ranked portraits of Classic winners, the sense of achievement is overwhelming. But so too, as we talked, is the cost of it. Not in money terms; although immaculate, this room is as Vogue magazine tasteful as the rest of the house. What has cost has been family as opposed to professional life. Picture-packed, video-stacked or not, the den could also seem a slightly lonely spot.

For all the public ebullience, the travelling-pack bustle of the racing circus, the hands-on devotion of assorted helpers down the years, the jockey's lot remains a singular one. When the talking's finished, it is only he in the saddle. Others will have prepared the horse, cleaned the kit, arranged the schedule. But in the end it comes down to one small man and a lot of large horses. Nothing else can matter. To get Willie Carson from Marija to the Maktoums nothing else could. That's always been the fact of it.

Or anyway, that's what he would have you believe. It was always going to be impossibly tough for the wee lad from Stirling and Middleham to climb the ladder against all the odds. No glittering early talent, no instant public recognition, not even for a long while any great sense of top-class self-belief. Just this incredible energy set on to the relentless treadmill of the racing scene. He likes to be brisk. 'You just have to get on with it,' he says. It's true and he has. He is not heavy into regrets. But that doesn't mean there hasn't been heartache along the way.

There were times when he hankered after an easier life, when he remembers his ambition having no great head for heights. Whatever the reality of that recollection the changes came and what has emerged from the mincer is an astonishingly well-organised one-man-band with a solid diamond of self-cen-tred determination at the heart of it. Maybe it's the only way to be. As with all solo performers, be they divas or discus throwers, life has to be made subservient to the talent. Then you get trophies in the den. But you also have the pictures you do not show.

There are all sorts of splendid memories on the walls. Horses like Troy, Sun Princess and Habibti; a fine oil painting of Dick Hern and Gordon Richards riding out on those West Ilsley downs. Then best of all there's a tremendous set-piece portrait of Willie aboard Minster Son, the horse he bred, standing in front of Minster House, the home he built; real fulfilment there. But the eye travels on across the snapshots. There's Willie and Elaine in hunting kit. There is the pair of them with friends in party mode. There are fun pictures of the Jack Russells, of assorted horses, of holiday shots. There are even now some playful snaps of the grandchildren who come to visit and to tumble over these so well tended chairs. But of their fathers, of Willie's three sons, there was not one picture here. The photo in this book of the young jockey playing football with his three boys on the lawns of Falmouth Cottage was very much of another time.

It has not been easy, it never is. He did not duck it as we talked. Read this and don't doubt the sadness there.　　U

When Carole and I were divorced it hit Tony, our eldest son, the hardest. He went off the rails a bit. He started rebelling and wasn't taking any interest in school. Carole's a soft person and he'd say he didn't want to go to school and that was that. She wasn't strong or strict enough with him. She was having such trouble with him that we decided to finish his schooling at fifteen and shove him off to Ireland, to Liam Browne, who we thought was a strict man and would sort him out.

He wanted to go into stables like his dad but it didn't quite work. He was all right for a while because he's a good worker when you can get him on the job. But he loses concentration quickly and isn't a hundred per cent reliable. He's still a bit like that though he has improved. He was with Liam for about a year, then he went to Clive Brittain. Clive was always a very supportive person to our family life. We lived next door to each other and I helped him a lot when he started training.

After that Tony went everywhere, spending shorter and shorter times at each place. He always let me down. I'd get him a job and he'd let me down. Neil did the same. I got him a job preparing yearlings and the day before he was due to start he decided he didn't want to do it. I was disappointed quite a few times and I ended up losing interest in them.

Then I got Ross into Radley with Dennis Silk, a lovely guy who bent over backwards for me to get the boy in. I thought it would make him. But he pulled the plug on me, too. He passed his O-levels with one A, a few Bs and Cs, so he was all right academically. And everybody liked him. His reports were fine. But then he decided he wanted to leave. I made him stay on for two more terms, but the last time he came home I just couldn't get him back. Everybody tried to make him stay: the other lads in the school, the head of the social club and Dennis Silk. But his mind was made up. I suspected him of being on drugs so I got Tony to find out what was going on. He said he didn't know but he insisted that there was no way Ross could be taking drugs because he didn't have any money. He ended up working in stables. But what he had developed was M.E. – it was a long time before they knew what was wrong with him.

He's the only one left with his mother and he's the one I have the least dealings with now. He's not a gentleman any more, he's reverted back. You wouldn't think he'd spent two or three years at Radley. Carole didn't agree with him going to boarding school in the first place. The only reason he went was because I demanded it in the divorce. I've often tried to talk to him about it but he just goes blank and says nothing. Perhaps in a way he's fulfilling his mother's wishes. He doesn't have any talent. He's riding now.

They're all stupid, the whole lot of them. None of them would listen to any advice that I gave them. Whether it was rebellion against me I don't know. But they wouldn't listen and in the end I gave up. I didn't think racing would be ideal for them, in fact I was hoping that if Ross was brainy enough he could have become a vet or something.

Tony's married now. There was a rough patch a while ago. I think he was messing round and she kicked him out. That didn't half straighten him up. They have two kids, one from the wife's first marriage. The kids are fun, but can sometimes be loathsome. I think what Tony missed was family life when he was a child. Now he's got these two kids he goes everywhere with them, really looks after them. He lives near Newmarket, works as a stable lad with Willie Jarvis. He's a good worker and might climb a bit higher. I suppose he's hoping to get something like second head lad. I get on well with him. He lends me his car whenever I want to go to Newmarket. And his wife, Janine, isn't bad.

Neil stayed with Chuck Spares, which was all a disaster. He got a few rides on bad horses. He was the only one who rode a winner on the Flat. He had a bit of talent but he was never going to go anywhere. It's a shame really that nobody moulded him, knocked him into shape. Then he had a year working in a printing business. When he left that he bought a farm just outside Newmarket. I was a bit unhappy about it. He married the daughter of a man called Gilbert, who was in transport to Italy. It's Gilbert's farm. They asked if I'd help them to buy it and I said yes, so they sent me a prospectus. When I read it I didn't fancy it much, but they still got it, so I think they were just having me on. I haven't seen the place so I don't know what it's actually like. They're into livery and breaking horses in. They have one kid, a daughter. I see them when they come down on their way to Devon and when I go up to Newmarket.

It's not a proper family, but I get on all right with them. The problem is that Carole and I had kids when we were too young. After all, we were only kids ourselves. I don't think we'll get closer now, unless some drama happens. Elaine gets on with them up to a point. But she doesn't really know them too well, especially Ross.

During the divorce my parents nearly took Carole's side to begin with. I was their son, so they had to support me, but they liked Carole. She is a very kind, generous person. But she had no pride in herself. I don't have any contact with her now, unless it's really necessary. As for Suzanne, well after the breakup there were a couple of rows, but things have calmed down now and we're friends. She's in California, married to a Mexican Indian. I think she's in real estate.

And there was my illegitimate daughter. I paid for her for years, until she was sixteen. I admitted it, it was taken to court and as a kid I had to pay twelve bob or something – I was only earning five quid a week. Every other year they tried to get more. I never denied it, but I decided right from the start that I was going to wash my hands of it. I suppose it was a shame for the kid, but I never saw her. I'm lucky in the sense that I've never had to go back to that area so the temptation to go and see her was never there. She's married now. I believe she sent a wedding invitation. I vaguely remember receiving it but it didn't click at first and I imagine Elaine chucked it in the bin. The next thing I knew was when I read about it on the front page of a newspaper.

SUMMING UP

Fulfilment, full circle or the end of the line? Come into the house, gaze out over the paddocks, look back into the rooms, and you are staring at success by the orchard full. From the Corton Estate, from the Middleham wash room, from Redcar's moving steeple, from Newmarket hopes to Leeds hospital disaster, all this has come. And not by chance. It has been brought by courage, by endless effort, and by design.

That last, once the least obvious, is now the most evident of all Willie Carson's attributes. At 50 he has a lifestyle unmatched by any grandfather in the land. Still competing at the highest level in one of the fastest and most violent of all our sports. Still a legend for crackling relentless energy throughout his public day. Yet so Scottishly tight with his private time that there is hardly a breath wasted as he gallops through another year.

Others of us tear around in circles at railway stations, chew up our patience in traffic jams and squander what sap is left on a hundred irrelevant things. Carson has got himself focused. He is a big-time jockey. His day, his beat, must fit this tune. Let's get it organised. Let's save the energy. Running over the moor to assignations in Leyburn, or trying to push John Forbes's car back from Catterick, were all a long, long time ago.

We are back in the conservatory. It's almost ten o'clock and breakfast was finished not much more than half an hour ago. There was a double racing shift yesterday, Brighton in the afternoon and Newbury in driving rain for the evening meeting. But a winner had come, the plane had made light of the Sussex leg, the night-time motorway return from Newbury took only 45 minutes in the big Toyota and the simple supper that Elaine served at the end of things had the gourmet touch of someone who began life as a professional in the kitchen.

Later today there will be another trip down to Brighton. 'Bilko', Alan Biltcliffe, the Biggles-moustached former Trident pilot, will have driven from his home near Broadway to collect the plane at Oxford and will then hop over to the airstrip by Ablington for Willie to take the controls all the way to the South Downs and that Shoreham descent over the turretted grandeur of Lancing College. The old airman will josh and moan at his chippy little pupil. With his head-set and lip-mike Carson will straddle the skies every bit as lively as Puck 'putting a girdle round about the earth' in Midsummer Night's Dream. Taken this way you turn the pressures of the job upside down. You would almost do it for the fun of travelling.

Not quite perhaps. At times like this Carson can look his years. The face can seem crumpled, there are clouds in those still extraordinarily wide blue eyes and you wonder about scars deeper than the famous zig zag on the left cheek. So much has been achieved but the riding cannot go on for ever. We are a few weeks away from the sunlit afternoon at Goodwood when the 3,500th winner had come up with a memorable triumph in the Stewards Cup. It was a landmark only previously passed by Gordon Richards and Lester Piggott. How many more milestones need to come?

That day had seen Willie at his finest. Not just in the dashing compulsive ride which stole the big race against the odds but in the masterly nursing effort which got a hesitant-looking partner home in the first. Whatever truth there was in the 'brute force and ignorance' jibe once levelled at his first championship year, has long since been confined to the dustbin. Carson now has a trademark. A little, hunched, unmistakable figure, clamped in behind the mane. Pushing and thinking and persuading with hands and body, and then with those backhanded slaps from either side. What happens when the dynamo runs down?   U

I've been quite pleased with my career. My record is very good. I've had my glory times. There were times when I thought I was as good as any, and I still get the feeling that if I have the horse I could get the job done. Dunfermline was the pinnacle at that time. Winning for the Queen was fantastic, being a royalist. I always regret not making more of that and really letting rip after the race – but I was involved with very conservative people so I tended to behave like them.

I don't have as much to do with Dick Hern now, but he is up against it. It has been very cruel for him recently. He's had to get used to new gallops and stables and has had bad luck, with a lot of coughing and the virus. The main thing is that he doesn't have the number of horses that he had before. In the first year it was all a bit makeshift – we thought we would muddle through, but the new stable hasn't had any rhythm to it. It hasn't worked and it's all a bit pathetic now.

You have years where it's all famine or feast. 1990 was a feast. It goes that way with owners, success seems to come and go. Nashwan's Derby was my biggest pay-day. I get nominations from Sheikh Hamdan, and Nashwan was syndicated for seventeen million. I have no standing arrangements, nothing in contract, it's all at the discretion of the owner, if he thinks I warrant it. I'm not on a lucrative retainer, but I get very well paid.

It's been depressing for me this year, with no real class horses to look forward to. John Dunlop hasn't got any, and Bashayer isn't up to the animals I've ridden before. I haven't seen much of the two-year-olds yet, but there are one or two rumblings in the pipeline. That's always the exciting time. As for agents, things went bad with Ted Eley ten years ago, it wasn't his fault. Elaine and I did it ourselves for a while, but Mike Cattermole's been my agent for four years now. Nice-mannered boy but hasn't got the feel for horses that he should have. He's very fair to everybody, in my eyes too fair, he could do with being a bit more cut-throat.

My career's had its lowlights as well, mainly getting sacked by different people. I remember Ray Laing once said I couldn't ride one of his at Sandown one day – his excuse was I wasn't strong enough. Not strong enough! Do you know who rode the three biggest Derby winners? Me. Henbit was 16.3 hands, Nashwan 16.2½ and Troy 16.2. All big horses and I rode them round Epsom, which is a very difficult course. A few other people haven't been happy with the way I've ridden horses, but most of the time it's not my ability but a preconceived idea about the animal or the race. I've got my opinions and they think my opinions wrong. One of my regrets is that I always say what I think and it is not always the best thing to do.

I don't think I have made many mistakes in the big races. I've made them in ordinary races, but I've never had an El Gran Senor. My worst ever would be Bashayer in the Cheshire Oaks this year. I got fined £1,200, and I don't agree with that. I didn't stop riding, just took it easy. Granted it was a mistake, but people who are found guilty of pulling horses intentionally only get £400.

It's only rarely that horses are stopped that could win. Saying a horse is 'not off' means it's not good enough to win the race, just running round for experience and to get fitter. If you think you can't win anyway you might take it easy, but if you're there with a chance of winning you'll be trying. Racing's not as bad as it looks. I was never one for stopping a horse that could win. Giving it an easy time is different, although my bottle used to go a bit. I have been on a horse and given orders to give it an easy ride but still come home to win. Too bad.

It happened once in Hong Kong, at Happy Valley. Betting's the game over there, waiting for the day when everything's right so they can really hit it, and on the other days hoping the jockey will ride the horse the wrong way. I was told to swing wide coming into the straight, so I did, but instead of dropping back the ground was so much faster out wide that I ended up going faster and faster and I won. There were pictures afterwards of me smiling and the owners leading the horse in with faces as long as fiddles.

For most of my career I've never been involved with betting stables. There was this one guy who used to train in Cheshire, only had one eye, and I rode a horse for him at Yarmouth. I didn't quite obey the orders, came up the middle of the course and won by a short head in a photo. He rushed out and asked me if I'd won. Course I bloody have, I said. I found out later that after the result this poor guy had got straight back in the car to go home, and first lay-by he came to he had to stop and was violently sick. He must have had his life savings on it, certainly more than he could really afford. I'm not a betting person. At one time you'd get all sorts of people and you'd give them what you thought would win, and they sort of gave you goods back – frozen meats from a butcher and things. I don't do that now.

Travelling to courses is much easier now I've got the plane. I've been flying for ten years. £120,000 the plane cost me. They're expensive toys – £30,000 a year running costs in all. You have to switch off from everything else when you're flying. You must concentrate. Listening to the talk-back on the radio most of the time, flight information. You go from station to station – Dunsfold to Shoreham, and they tell you what frequency it is although you should know these things before you take off. Route marked on the map and all the frequencies at your fingertips. When you have controlled airspace you have to ask the station to go on their levels or through their zone. You tell them what your intentions are and what height you want and they'll say yes or no, tell you to change height or steer you round another plane.

I'm very proud of this house. All the doors are made by a carpenter. The stairs are softwood, the banisters are all oak, and the panels in the kitchen. I've collected wood for years – the table's my favourite mahogany. In the wood outside I have a partridge, two cock pheasants, and a white hen, but I haven't seen her for a while. She might have been gobbled. I have a fox, with definitely one cub, maybe more. We had a red deer running up and down by the garden fence the other day, he must have escaped from somewhere, and there are lots of fallow deer on the meadow.

I bought the stud a few years ago, when it was quite run down. Buying and setting it up cost £140,000, a lot of money in those days. I'm still doing it up. There are ten mares in at the moment. It's quite a big stud, and I could take in more but there's already the young stock and cattle to look after. I employ two men. I actually hate racing starting because there is so much happening at that time in the stud, with mares being bought and foals being born. All sorts of work to do – mucking out, cattle, tractors, fence-mending, hedge-cutting, fertilising. Stud turnover is in six figures, and it's hard to judge a profit but it does run at a profit. I've tried to get things all set up so it will tick over for the next ten years without any fresh input. I'd like to take in a stallion, top quality blood without buying at an expensive price. I had my eye on a three-year-old a few years back, who turned out to be none other than

Dayjur. Then earlier this year I fancied Hamas, but now he's won the July Cup I won't get him either.

You can't go on forever as a jockey. The body won't take it. You keep having accidents, and they are catching up on me. I haven't any one set thing that I would do when I retire. I have got the stud, but that won't take a lot of running and is more of a winter job. If I ever started training, it would be on a very low key. I don't think I could try to build up a yard, but if someone offered me to take over a ready-made set-up that would be a different thing altogether.

When people know what they are going to do when they retire they go early. Perhaps I am going on longer than I should because I don't know what else to do. One day I'll just say, that's it. The unknown. You try to prepare yourself for it, but it's going to be a bit boring.

CONCLUSION

He gets up, still a wonderfully spruce little figure in tailored slacks and stylish, blue-and-white Shadwell Stud sweat shirt. He walks out to show you the garden and you try and take in how he would handle a life without the riding treadmill which has run it and enriched it for as long as most of us can remember. There is a bronze of Troy in the oak-panelled central hall from which all the other rooms run. Elaine comes down those elegantly banistered stairs which add an almost eighteenth-century touch to this very twentieth-century home. The portable phone goes and Willie picks it up on the move. It's about a ride. What will happen when it doesn't ring again?

We go out through the back storeroom where his mother is clearing some boxes and putting the dog back through the door. Even in her late seventies May Carson is still one of the wonders of the world. A tiny, bustling Scottish hen bird, there's never been any doubt where Willie got his energy from. Her son scolds her about something. 'Och, you never get any rest,' she says to us teasingly, 'not if you are Billy Carson's mum.'

The little man himself likes to keep up his grudging 'they have got to keep useful' image, but you more than suspect that he is inordinately proud of having his parents set up across the fields in one of the cottages of his stud. The returned devotion from both them and his now Cambridgeshire-based sister Elizabeth is almost warm to the touch.

We walked across the grass to where Elaine is tending the newly installed and marvellously equipped duck pond complete with island nesting boxes and a single electric wire to deter the local fox from even thinking of jumping the meshed perimeter fence. Elaine talks enthusiastically about the assorted wildfowl which are already sculling about the pond. There's a mandarin duck, a Chiloe wigeon and a Bahama pintail. These are special birds. This is collector's chat. They are difficult to breed from but over on the far side some wooden boxes house some broody hens bidding to hatch out a new ornamental generation.

Willie steps carefully through the rushes, lifts the nesting box roof and pushes the fussing hen aside with a countryman's ease. 'Listen,' he says as a distant cheeping comes from somewhere deep inside, 'I think there's an egg cracking right this instant.'

The intent face famous from so many thousand finishes was really focused now. The boyish enthusiasm from all those TV interviews was unchecked and uncontrived. Willie Carson's blue eyes went wide with wonder as the little gooey cobwebby beak struggled out to start life as a northern pintail. 'What a cracker,' he said. 'We were there right on time.'

As we walked back towards the house, the car, and the plane to Brighton, the sun was dappling the mares and foals in the paddock beyond the rails. It was very, very England but yet there was something familiar about Willie's talk that took you further north and long ago. Then you had it. We were back in grandfather's time. Messing about with the pigeon loft, the sheep, the goats down by the Abbey and that trotter which had given Willie the very first ride of all. Those were riches then, these were prizes now. Only the birds have changed.

This is where the rainbow ends.

Or does it?   U

WILLIE CARSON'S TOP TWENTY

If this was on home work alone, Admiral's Launch would rate just below Nashwan and Dayjur. He was stunning on the gallops, but he never reproduced it on the track. Anyway, just to get you all arguing, here in order are my top twenty horses.

1. DAYJUR

He was all muscle. When you thought about passing a horse you had passed it. It was a pleasure to get out of bed in the morning to ride this horse. When you'd finished, you were tingling. He ran twice as a two-year-old, won first time and got beat the second, when he was making a bit of noise and I thought something was wrong with his wind. So he was hobdayed. But then again I was riding him wrong, and I didn't find that out until we got beaten at Newbury by Tod. We knew he was fast so we were trying to restrain him and we didn't get the speed at the finish. When we changed tactics and let him run from the front he was brilliant. The fastest horse I've ever ridden. As for America, well in my own mind I think we won that too.

2. NASHWAN

Nash the Dash. He won at Newbury at two, not impressively but well enough, then won at Ascot. He didn't show any brilliance at two, but he was good. He had a lot of furnishing to come – it was like buying a car with no seats in it. At three he had a splint and missed a lot of work, and it wasn't until Prince of Dance went wrong that Nash was asked a question because his preparation had just been steady work until then, though he'd done it brilliantly. The first time I was allowed to sit on him and have a feel it was electrifying. And then we had the big gallop. Without a doubt the most exciting gallop I've ever had. It was special. We knew then he'd win the Guineas. I did doubt whether he'd get the trip in the Derby and in fact he didn't quite get home, I remember him wandering and hitting the fence just before the winning line. After the King George the brilliance at home waned. He wasn't sparkling, though there was one bit of work just before he went to France when I thought he was coming back. The form of the race he got beat in isn't that bad – he was trying to give seven pounds to Group One winners, and he'd still have won at level weights despite not really liking the ground. The hype about this horse was unbelievable. He gave me a lot of fun. And I believed in him.

3. TROY

A giant of a horse, looked like a Leicestershire hunter. I remember the Royal Lodge run. The top horse at the time was Lyphard's Wish, a front-runner. I rode Troy up behind him hoping to get past him but he couldn't do it, and Ela-Mana-Mou came from way off the pace to beat us. I learned that Troy couldn't be taken too fast, he needed time. It taught me to be very patient with him. He was a galloper but he just needed time to build up momentum. What I learned in that race won the Derby for me. He came out at three to win at Sandown, only by a neck but he was running a bit green as I'd taken him down the centre of the course on his own for better ground. Then he won the Predominate, which was my first ride back after ten days off with a broken collarbone – I was in pain but I had to ride him. In the Derby they went very fast and coming down the hill I was so far back I was thinking never mind, there'll be another year. Then he picked up at Tattenham Corner and started grabbing the ground and I thought we might get close. Then he got to the front and I thought, we'll win. We won by seven lengths, and it was a good year that year, lots of good horses. In the King George he beat the Irish, beat the French, and then went on and won at York over a mile and a quarter although everything happened a bit quick for him and he had to work. Then in the Arc the ground came up too soft for him and he could only manage a place. Troy was a big, gentle giant, one of those horses you were quite at ease with because he galloped and was always better than the rest. He never seemed to smile, he just went about his business with a deadpan face. One thing he did that used to worry me was whipping round on the gallops. I used to worry that I'd fall off – I didn't, though. Couldn't really, not with him being worth so much.

4. Sun Princess

One of the most brilliant animals you could ever ride, but unmanageable, everything was an argument. The more you pulled at her the more she'd fight. At two and in her first race at three I rode her very gently, trying not to get aggressive or upset her, almost not trying at all. The most important thing was to get her to relax. In the Oaks she was still a maiden, and she won by twelve lengths. I got fed up holding her! I let her go coming down the hill, and she was away. She was a strong filly. In the Yorkshire Oaks there were only four runners, and the other three were planning to go slow because they thought I would have trouble holding her, but I surprised them all by jumping out and making the running. That spoiled her, because from then on she always wanted to jump off in front. She won the Leger with the soft ground helping us, and I thought I had the Arc won but All Along came and beat us. Working her could be difficult. Once we took her to Bath to exercise before a big race. As soon as we got on the track off she went on a circuit of the course. She had some work but not the kind we wanted to give her! Then we tried to work her at Newbury in behind a horse called His Honour but that didn't work either. She clambered all over him so much that she severed his tendon and he never ran again.

5. Salsabil

A very feminine filly, perfect size for a racehorse. After she'd been beaten as a two-year-old she won over in France. When she won the Fred Darling by a mile people were falling over themselves to take a price for the Guineas. All the hype took me a bit by surprise, because although she'd won well I couldn't understand why people were getting all hyped up. They knew her better than I did. She won the Guineas well, very straight forward. I thought it was a bad decision to run her in the Oaks, but there you are. Then she went and won the Irish Derby. The easiest Classic winner I've ever ridden, everything went right. She won the Vermeille after a lay-off but ran out of road in the Arc. She just wasn't right.

6. HENBIT

A very brave horse, and a very big horse too. 16.3 hands, the tallest Derby winner ever. His stride was the most important thing about him, he got over a lot of ground. He could handle bends well, too – won very impressively round the tight course at Chester – because although he was tall he wasn't heavy. He gave me such a great feel at Chester that I thought he was bound to win the Derby. That he did so with what amounted to a broken leg made him very special to me. That is why he is rated so highly.

7. KNOWN FACT

I inherited this horse from Lester because he was a bolter, he would bolt in his races. The first time I rode him I put his head over the rails to stop him running away, and he finished fourth. Then we won the Middle Park, and I remember saying to Humphrey Cottrill, who managed Khalid Abdullah's horses at the time, the horse is a gift. He won the Guineas slightly by default, although he was only beaten a neck all the same. Then he went on to win the Queen Elizabeth, which was a great race. Known Fact and Kris, one of the most gigantic battles. Everything went right for me and I just went past the other one.

8. ROSE BOWL

She was a brilliant filly, fantastic turn of foot. I always remember when you asked her to quicken, she would quicken and go lower to the ground like a Citroen when you get out of it. Lester rode her before I did and would overdo the waiting tactics. I used to go on her about two out. She galloped like a deer or a whippet, her back legs came in front of her front legs. You don't see that very often.

9. PETOSKI

What I remember about Petoski is having dinner in my little cottage in West Ilsley with James Bethell the night before the King George. He hadn't run brilliantly in the Derby and James said I had no chance of beating Oh So Sharp, but he had been working so well I was virtually confident of victory. After we'd won the race we were going for York, and I remember riding work on him beforehand and he'd improved again. I was over the moon, it was fantastic work. I thought the horse was going to be one of the greats, he was improving so much. Then he broke a bone. We kept him in training but he was never the same again.

10. DUNFERMLINE

I was never very impressed with her. She wasn't a feminine animal, didn't have much character, not good-looking either. But her Oaks was at that time the biggest day of my life, a great feeling winning for Her Majesty. The Leger was a tactical triumph although I worried at one stage when I thought I wouldn't catch Lester. Then she was unlucky in the Arc – the pace wasn't strong enough for me and I couldn't do anything about it. It was a tactical error, and possibly with hindsight we should have made the running.

11. HABIBTI

She kept winning by long margins and she was good, but she was also lucky. She came up against a poor crop of sprinters and always had Soba to make the pace for her. She just kept on winning for us at three, although she lost her way at four. She didn't stay in the Guineas but won all the top sprints. A very good filly.

12. HIGH TOP

He was a very unlucky horse, he only won two races as a three-year-old – the Thirsk trial and the Guineas. It was a terrible day when he won the Guineas, the most miserable I've ridden in. He was galloping into a gale, and there was water everywhere. It was always the plan to go all the way on him. He was a great galloper, a very strong horse.

13. BIREME

She came at a time when we had a lot of good fillies. We had three in the Oaks, and it was the biggest decision I ever had to make. There was The Dancer, and Shoot A Line, who never got beaten that year, apart from at Epsom. Bireme was a filly who was very manly, a big, strapping filly, a galloper. She went in front at the turn in the Oaks but she could have made all the running. Galloping came easy to her. After the Oaks she had leg trouble and never ran again.

14. ELA-MANA-MOU

He came to us from Guy Harwood's. He was a miniature horse, very strong. We learned early on that he hated the firm ground. Brave, brave, brave little horse. His King George was an instinctive race by me, I went to the front when the horse wanted to go, about half a mile out. I knew he'd stay. He was gallant, genuine, a little body but a big heart.

15. MINSTER SON

The horse I bred. He only got beat in the Derby as a three-year-old. His form was fantastic and I don't think he got the credit he deserved. He was a very, very brave horse. Every time he ran he had to have rests for two or three weeks, and he had to go through a lot of excessive work quickly to get him fit. I remember him as a foal and a yearling, he was always a nervous and arrogant horse. I usually sit on yearlings before they go to the sales but Minster Son was one I didn't sit on. He was a bit of a boy.

16. DIBIDALE

A very unfortunate filly, she had a tragic career. She hadn't much brilliance, but she was a great, dour galloper. The Oaks misfortune was well-documented. She was a very deep-chested filly, and the girths just slipped. The reins began to get longer round Tattenham Corner and I realised I'd fall off so I jumped onto her back – I don't know if I could do that now! All I wanted to do was win the race, I only realised the weightcloth had gone after Tony Murray had helped me pull up, and I was so annoyed I thwacked the ground with my whip. After the Oaks, she came and won the Irish Oaks, turning the Epsom form right around. Then she lost her life in a race at Newbury. Frankie Durr's horse kicked us up the backside and she went down, split a pastern. They tried to save her by putting it in plaster but she had to be put down.

17. BOLDBOY

This was the one they said I'd never be able to ride, and I ended up winning a string of races on him. He got more temperamental as he got older and pulled hard, but he wasn't too difficult to ride. You couldn't hit him, though. If you hit him he stopped, so it was always hands and heels. He was a big, strong horse. One day at York he was fantastic, he gave me a real thrill, one of those races that just sticks in your mind.

18. SHADAYID

She was brilliant in her early career. She was quite a hot filly, never made things easy for me. She was like a naughty little girl, you had to grab hold of her all the time. She was very talented. But then we ran her in the Oaks and she didn't get home, and that finished her. Her enthusiasm waned and she never really recovered.

19. PRINCE OF DANCE

He was possibly better than Nashwan. We always thought he was. We thought he could win the Triple Crown. He had a problem with his spinal cord. We didn't know about it as a two-year-old but it affected his preparation for the Guineas. His first few pieces of work at three were brilliant. But then it all went wrong.

20. DON'T FORGET ME

He was a good-looking, imposing horse. This was at the time when things were going badly for me and no-one wanted to put me up. I was at Thurles in Ireland in the winter and begged this horse's owners to let me ride him. Eventually, after five other jockeys couldn't, I got the ride. He was a great front-runner, just kept on getting better. He was a fantastic horse on his day and his times in the Guineas were brilliant, but he didn't do much after the Irish Guineas.

WILLIE CARSON FACTFILE

Full name: William Fisher Hunter Carson
Born: Stirling, 16 November 1942
Father: Tom Carson (warehouseman)
Apprenticeship: Gerald Armstrong, Middleham 1958-62; Sam Armstrong, Newmarket, 1962-65
First ride: Marija (Gerald Armstrong), 5th at Redcar, 18 May 1959
First win: Pinkers Pond (Gerald Armstrong), Catterick, 19 July 1962
First big win: Monkey Palm (Sam Armstrong), 1965 Great St Wilfrid Handicap
Lost claim: Regal Bell (Sam Armstrong), Redcar, 3 August 1965
First Derby mount: Laureate (Bernard van Cutsem), 11th in 1968
First win at Royal Ascot: Celtic Cone (Bernard van Cutsem), 1971 Ascot Stakes
First Group 1 win: Sharpen Up (Bernard van Cutsem), 1971 Middle Park Stakes
First Classic win: High Top (Bernard van Cutsem), 1972 2,000 Guineas
Six wins on one card: Newcastle, 30 June 1990 (from 7 rides)
Five wins on one card: Redcar, 7 August 1976 (from 5 rides)
Most serious injury: fractured skull in fall from Silken Knot, York, 18 August 1981
2,000th win in Britain: Busaco, Newmarket, 26 June 1982
3,000th win in Britain: Kawtuban, Salisbury, 22 May 1990
3,500th win in Britain: King's Signet, Goodwood (Stewards' Cup), 31 July 1993
Main retainers: Lord Derby/Bernard van Cutsem 1967-75, Clive Brittain 1976, Dick Hern 1977-89, Hamdan al Maktoum from 1990
Champion jockey: 5 times—1972, 1973, 1978, 1980, 1983
Most wins in a British season: 187 in 1990
Number of centuries in a British season: 21 (up to start of 1993)
Horses of the Year: Troy (1979), Habibti (1983), Nashwan (1989), Dayjur (1990)
English Classic wins: 16 (up to St Leger, 1993)
Classic winner as breeder: Minster Son, 1988 St Leger
Triple Crown winner: Longboat, 1986 Stayers' Triple Crown
Richest win: Flying Brave, 1990 Tattersalls Tiffany Highflyer Stakes (Newmarket)

RECORD IN BRITAIN 1962-92

	Won		2nd	3rd	Rides
1962	1		1	3	26
1963	5		6	5	79
1964	15		7	13	131
1965	37		40	22	318
1966	35		30	26	333
1967	35		35	38	372
1968	61	(9)	46	39	424
1969	66	(10)	44	41	468
1970	86	(3)	73	87	699
1971	145	(2)	108	100	795
1972	132	(1)	121	100	829
1973	164	(1)	126	98	883
1974	129	(4)	143	96	908
1975	131	(2)	128	109	849
1976	138	(2)	142	106	865
1977	160	(2)	138	102	892
1978	182	(1)	143	113	986
1979	142	(2)	123	82	820
1980	166	(1)	135	109	852
1981	114	(2)	82	75	576
1982	145	(2)	124	87	827
1983	159	(1)	90	98	732
1984	97	(5)	106	99	676
1985	125	(3)	134	110	832
1986	130	(3)	115	109	831
1987	100	(4)	130	85	782
1988	130	(2)	100	87	832
1989	138	(3)	125	121	867
1990	187	(2)	131	103	906
1991	155	(2)	130	93	890
1992	125	(3)	120	107	856
TOTAL	3,435		2,976	2,463	21,136

In brackets: position in jockeys' table

N.B. The jockeys' title is traditionally decided on the number of wins but Carson was top jockey in the amount of prize-money earned in 1989, 1990 and 1991.

CARSON'S BEST MOUNTS *(Timeform ratings)*

		Trainer	Owner

COLTS

		Trainer	Owner
137	* Troy 1979 (3yr)	Dick Hern	Sir Michael Sobell
	* Dayjur 1990 (3yr)	Dick Hern	Hamdan al Maktoum
135	Known Fact 1980 (3yr)	Jeremy Tree	Prince Khalid Abdullah
	Petoski 1985 (3yr)	Dick Hern	Dowager Lady Beaverbrook
	* Nashwan 1989 (3yr)	Dick Hern	Hamdan al Maktoum
132	Bay Express 1975 (4yr)	Peter Nelson	P A V Cooper
	Ela-Mana-Mou 1980 (4yr)	Dick Hern	Simon Weinstock
	Gorytus 1982 (2yr)	Dick Hern	Mrs Alice duPont Mills
131	High Top 1971 (2yr)	Bernard van Cutsem	Sir Jules Thorn
	Relkino 1977 (4yr)	Dick Hern	Dowager Lady Beaverbrook
	Unfuwain 1988 (3yr)	Dick Hern	Hamdan al Maktoum
130	Parnell 1972 (4yr) & 1973 (5yr)	Bernard van Cutsem	Roderic More O'Ferrall
	Homing 1978 (3yr)	Dick Hern	Lord Rotherwick
	Henbit 1980 (3yr)	Dick Hern	Mme Etti Plesch
	Minster Son 1988 (3yr)	Neil Graham (Dick Hern)	Dowager Lady Beaverbrook

FILLIES

		Trainer	Owner
136	* Habibti 1983 (3yr)	John Dunlop	Mohammed Mutawa
133	Rose Bowl 1975 (3yr)	Fulke Johnson Houghton	Mrs Jane Englehard
	Dunfermline 1977 (3yr)	Dick Hern	The Queen
130	Awaasif 1982 (3yr)	John Dunlop	Sheikh Mohammed
	Sun Princess 1983 (3yr)	Dick Hern	Sir Michael Sobell
	Salsabil 1990 (3yr)	John Dunlop	Hamdan al Maktoum
129	Dibidale 1974 (3yr)	Barry Hills	Nick Robinson
127	Bireme 1980 (3yr)	Dick Hern	Dick Hollingsworth
	Shoot A Line 1980 (3yr)	Dick Hern	Alan Budgett

GELDINGS

		Trainer	Owner
126	Boldboy 1977 (7yr)	Dick Hern	Dowager Lady Beaverbrook
125	Bedtime 1984 (4yr)	Dick Hern	Lord Halifax
122	Teleprompter 1984 (4yr)	Bill Watts	Lord Derby

*Horse of the Year

CARSON'S ENGLISH CLASSIC WINNERS

	Trainer	Owner
2,000 GUINEAS		
1972 High Top	Bernard van Cutsem	Sir Jules Thorn
1980 Known Fact	Jeremy Tree	Prince Khalid Abdullah
1987 Don't Forget Me	Richard Hannon	Jim Horgan
1989 Nashwan	Dick Hern	Hamdan al Maktoum
1,000 GUINEAS		
1990 Salsabil	John Dunlop	Hamdan al Maktoum
1991 Shadayid	John Dunlop	Hamdan al Maktoum
DERBY		
1979 Troy	Dick Hern	Sir Michael Sobell
1980 Henbit	Dick Hern	Mme Etti Plesch
1989 Nashwan	Dick Hern	Hamdan al Maktoum
OAKS		
1977 Dunfermline	Dick Hern	The Queen
1980 Bireme	Dick Hern	Dick Hollingsworth
1983 Sun Princess	Dick Hern	Sir Michael Sobell
1990 Salsabil	John Dunlop	Hamdan al Maktoum
ST LEGER		
1977 Dunfermline	Dick Hern	The Queen
1983 Sun Princess	Dick Hern	Sir Michael Sobell
1988 Minster Son	Neil Graham (Dick Hern)	Dowager Lady Beaverbrook

CLASSIC-PLACED MOUNTS

2,000 Guineas: Noble Decree (2nd 1973), Bairn (2nd 1985), Charmer (2nd 1988)

1,000 Guineas: Habibti (3rd 1983)

Derby: Hot Grove (2nd 1977), Elmaamul (3rd 1990), Marju (2nd 1991)

Oaks: Aureoletta (3rd 1973), Val's Girl (2nd 1975), Roses For The Star (2nd 1976), Bonnie Isle (2nd 1979), Three Tails (3rd 1987), Roseate Tern (2nd 1989), Shadayid (3rd 1991)

St Leger: Libra's Rib (3rd 1975), Niniski (3rd 1979), Water Mill (2nd 1980), Dry Dock (3rd 1987), Roseate Tern (3rd 1989) Hellenic (2nd 1990)

CARSON'S FOREIGN CLASSIC WINNERS

	Trainer	Owner
IRISH 2,000 GUINEAS		
1987 Don't Forget Me	Richard Hannon	Jim Horgan
IRISH DERBY		
1979 Troy	John Dunlop	Sir Michael Sobell
1990 Salsabil	John Dunlop	Hamdan al Maktoum
IRISH OAKS		
1974 Dibidale	Barry Hills	Nick Robinson
1980 Shoot A Line	Dick Hern	Alan Budgett
1982 Swiftfoot	Dick Hern	Lord Rotherwick
1985 Helen Stree	Dick Hern	Sir Michael Sobell
IRISH ST LEGER		
1979 Niniski	Dick Hern	Dowager Lady Beaverbrook
PRIX DU JOCKEY-CLUB		
1980 Policeman	Charlie Milbank	Fred Tinsley
PRIX DE DIANE		
1990 Rafha	Henry Cecil	Prince Faisal
PRIX ROYAL-OAK		
1979 Niniski	Dick Hern	Dowager Lady Beaverbrook
PREMIO PARIOLI		
1992 Alhijaz	John Dunlop	Prince Faisal
DERBY ITALIANO		
1976 Red Arrow	A Pandolfi	Scuderia Diamante
1986 Tommy Way	John Dunlop	Scuderia Erasec
OAKS D'ITALIA		
1985 Miss Gris	Alduino Botti	Scuderia Siba

CARSON'S DERBY MOUNTS

		Place	Trainer
1968	Laureate	11th	Bernard van Cutsem
1969	Backing Britain	19th	Arthur Goodwill
1971	Meaden	9th	Barry Hills
1972	Meadow Mint	10th	Sam Armstrong
1973	Ksar	4th	Bernard van Cutsem
1974	Court Dancer	9th	Paul Cole
1975	Royal Manacle	7th	Barry Hills
1976	Tierra Fuego	11th	Clive Brittain
1977	Hot Grove	2nd	Fulke Johnson Houghton
1978	Admiral's Launch	12th	Dick Hern
1979	TROY	WON	Dick Hern
1980	HENBIT	WON	Dick Hern
1981	Church Parade	5th	Dick Hern
1982	Jalmood	14th	John Dunlop
1983	Morcon	8th	Dick Hern
1984	Kaytu	8th	Dick Hern
1985	Petoski	11th	Dick Hern
1986	Sharrood	8th	Dick Hern
1987	Love the Groom	12th	John Dunlop
1988	Minster Son	8th	Dick Hern
1989	NASHWAN	WON	Dick Hern
1990	Elmaamul	3rd	Dick Hern
1991	Marju	2nd	John Dunlop
1992	Muhtarram	4th	John Gosden
1993	Cairo Prince	4th	Peter Chapple-Hyam

CARSON'S KING GEORGE MOUNTS

		Place	Trainer
1972	Parnell	2nd	Bernard van Cutsem
1973	Parnell	5th	Bernard van Cutsem
1975	Dibidale	7th	Barry Hills
1976	Coin of Gold	6th	Clive Brittain
1978	Dunfermline	8th	Dick Hern
1979	TROY	WON	Dick Hern
1980	ELA-MANA-MOU	WON	Dick Hern
1982	Height of Fashion	7th	Dick Hern
1983	Sun Princess	3rd	Dick Hern
1985	PETOSKI	WON	Dick Hern
1986	Petoski	6th	Dick Hern
1988	Unfuwain	2nd	Dick Hern
1989	NASHWAN	WON	Dick Hern
1990	Husyan	8th	Peter Walwyn
1991	Sapience	5th	Jimmy FitzGerald
1992	Saddlers' Hall	2nd	Michael Stoute
1993	Tenby	8th	Henry Cecil

CARSON'S ARC DE TRIOMPHE MOUNTS

		Place	Trainer
1971	One For All	9th	Horatio Luro
1972	Parnell	9th	Bernard van Cutsem
1973	Parnell	18th	Bernard van Cutsem
1974	Proverb	14th	Barry Hills
1977	Dunfermline	4th	Dick Hern
1978	Exdirectory	17th	Paddy Prendergast
1979	Troy	3rd	Dick Hern
1980	Ela-Mana-Mou	3rd	Dick Hern
1982	Awaasif	3rd	John Dunlop
1983	Sun Princess	2nd	Dick Hern
1984	Sun Princess	9th	Dick Hern
1985	Killiniski	11th	John Dunlop
1988	Unfuwain	4th	Neil Graham (Dick Hern)
1990	Salsabil	10th	John Dunlop
1992	Saddlers' Hall	15th	Michael Stoute

CARSON'S GROUP 1 WINS

1971

Middle Park Stakes	Sharpen Up	Bernard van Cutsem	Mrs Mimi van Cutsem
Observer Gold Cup	High Top	Bernard van Cutsem	Sir Jules Thorn

1972

2,000 Guineas	High Top	Bernard van Cutsem	Sir Jules Thorn
Preis von Europa	Prince Ippi	Theo Grieper	Gestüt Röttgen

1973

Gran Premio d'Italia	Prince Ippi	Theo Grieper	Gestüt Röttgen

1974

Irish Oaks	Dibidale	Barry Hills	Nick Robinson
Yorkshire Oaks	Dibidale	Barry Hills	Nick Robinson

1975

Champion Stakes	Rose Bowl	Fulke Johnson Houghton	Mrs Jane Engelhard
Prix de la Foret	Roan Star	Roger Poincelet	Mme H Lazar

1976

Derby Italiano	Red Arrow	A Pandolfi	Scuderia Diamante
Grosser Preis von Baden	Sharper	A Hecker	A von Kaick
Flying Childers Stakes	Mandrake Major	Denys Smith	John Van Geest

1977

Oaks Stakes	Dunfermline	Dick Hern	The Queen
Benson & Hedges Gold Cup	Relkino	Dick Hern	Dowager Lady Beaverbrook
St Leger Stakes	Dunfermline	Dick Hern	The Queen

1978

Grosser Preis von Berlin	First Lord	G Zuber	S Weissenhof

1979

Derby Stakes	Troy	Dick Hern	Sir Michael Sobell
Irish Derby	Troy	Dick Hern	Sir Michael Sobell
King George VI & Queen Elizabeth Stakes	Troy	Dick Hern	Sir Michael Sobell
Benson & Hedges Gold Cup	Troy	Dick Hern	Sir Michael Sobell
Middle Park Stakes	Known Fact	Jeremy Tree	Prince Khalid Abdullah
Irish St Leger	Niniski	Dick Hern	Dowager Lady Beaverbrook
Prix Royal-Oak	Niniski	Dick Hern	Dowager Lady Beaverbrook

1980

2,000 Guineas	Known Fact	Jeremy Tree	Prince Khalid Abdullah
Derby Stakes	Henbit	Dick Hern	Mme Etti Plesch
Oaks Stakes	Bireme	Dick Hern	Dick Hollingsworth
Prix du Jockey-Club	Policeman	Charlie Milbank	Fred Tinsley
Eclipse Stakes	Ela-Mana-Mou	Dick Hern	Simon Weinstock
Irish Oaks	Shoot a Line	Dick Hern	Alan Budgett
King George VI & Queen Elizabeth Stakes	Ela-Mana-Mou	Dick Hern	Simon Weinstock

1982

Irish Oaks	Swiftfoot	Dick Hern	Lord Rotherwick
Prix Morny	Deep Roots	Pascal Bary	Mme P Barbe
Prix de la Salamandre	Deep Roots (dead-heat)	Pascal Bary	Mme P Barbe

1983

Premio Presidente della Repubblica	Jalmood	John Dunlop	Sheikh Mohammed
Gran Premio d'Italia	Celio Rufo	Luigi Camici	Scuderia Erasec
Oaks Stakes	Sun Princess	Dick Hern	Sir Michael Sobell
Gold Cup	Little Wolf	Dick Hern	Lord Porchester
July Cup	Habibti	John Dunlop	Mohammed Mutawa
Yorkshire Oaks	Sun Princess	Dick Hern	Sir Michael Sobell
St Leger Stakes	Sun Princess	Dick Hern	Sir Michael Sobell

Prix de L'Abbaye	Habibti	John Dunlop	Mohammed Mutawa
Premio Roma	High Hawk	John Dunlop	Sheikh Mohammed

1984

King's Stand Stakes	Habibti	John Dunlop	Mohammed Mutawa
Yorkshire Oaks	Circus Plume	John Dunlop	Sir Robin McAlpine

1985

Oaks d'Italia	Miss Gris	Alduino Botti	Scuderia Siba
Irish Oaks	Helen Street	Dick Hern	Sir Michael Sobell
King George VI & Queen Elizabeth Stakes	Petoski	Dick Hern	Dowager Lady Beaverbrook

1986

Derby Italiano	Tommy Way	John Dunlop	Scuderia Erasec
Gran Premio di Milano	Tommy Way	John Dunlop	Scuderia Erasec
Gold Cup	Longboat	Dick Hern	Dick Hollingsworth
Gran Criterium	Sanam	John Dunlop	Prince Faisal

1987

2,000 Guineas	Don't Forget Me	Richard Hannon	Jim Horgan
Irish 2,000 Guineas	Don't Forget Me	Richard Hannon	Jim Horgan
Prix Marcel Boussac	Ashayer	John Dunlop	Hamdan al Maktoum
Futurity Stakes	Emmson	Dick Hern	Sir Michael Sobell

1988

International Stakes	Shady Heights	Robert Armstrong	George Tong
St Leger Stakes	Minster Son	Neil Graham (Dick Hern)	Dowager Lady Beaverbrook
Dewhurst Stakes	Prince of Dance (dead-heat)	Neil Graham (Dick Hern)	Sir Michael Sobell
Prix de la Foret	Salse	Henry Cecil	Sheikh Mohammed
Futurity Stakes	Al Hareb	Neil Graham (Dick Hern)	Hamdan al Maktoum

1989

2,000 Guineas	Nashwan	Dick Hern	Hamdan al Maktoum
Premio Presidente della Repubblica	Alwuhush	John Dunlop	Hamdan al Maktoum
Derby Stakes	Nashwan	Dick Hern	Hamdan al Maktoum
Gran Premio di Milano	Alwuhush	John Dunlop	Hamdan al Maktoum

Gold Cup	Sadeem	Guy Harwood	Sheikh Mohammed
Eclipse Stakes	Nashwan	Dick Hern	Hamdan al Maktoum
King George VI & Queen Elizabeth Stakes	Nashwan	Dick Hern	Hamdan al Maktoum
Yorkshire Oaks	Roseate Tern	Dick Hern	Lord Carnarvon
Prix Marcel Boussac	Salsabil	Dick Hern	Hamdan al Maktoum
Premio Roma	Highland Chieftain	Dick Hern	David Hunisett

1990

1,000 Guineas	Salsabil	John Dunlop	Hamdan al Maktoum
Oaks Stakes	Salsabil	John Dunlop	Hamdan al Maktoum
Prix de Diane	Rafha	Henry Cecil	Prince Faisal
Irish Derby	Salsabil	Dick Hern	Hamdan al Maktoum
Eclipse Stakes	Elmaamul	Dick Hern	Hamdan al Maktoum
Sussex Stakes	Distant Relative	Barry Hills	Wafic Said
Yorkshire Oaks	Hellenic	Dick Hern	Lord Weinstock
Nunthorpe Stakes	Dayjur	Dick Hern	Hamdan al Maktoum
Phoenix Champion Stakes	Elmaamul	Dick Hern	Hamdan al Maktoum
Haydock Sprint Cup	Dayjur	Dick Hern	Hamdan al Maktoum
Prix Vermeille	Salsabil	John Dunlop	Hamdan al Maktoum
Prix Marcel Boussac	Shadayid	John Dunlop	Hamdan al Maktoum
Prix de L'Abbaye	Dayjur	Dick Hern	Hamdan al Maktoum

1991

1,000 Guineas	Shadayid	John Dunlop	Hamdan al Maktoum
St James Palace Stakes	Marju	John Dunlop	Hamdan al Maktoum
Middle Park Stakes	Rodrigo de Triano	Peter Chapple-Hyam	Robert Sangster
Dewhurst Stakes	Dr Devious	Peter Chapple-Hyam	Luciano Gaucci

1992

Premio Parioli	Alhijaz	John Dunlop	Prince Faisal
Premio Vittorio di Capua	Alhijaz	John Dunlop	Prince Faisal
Queen Elizabeth II Stakes	Lahib	John Dunlop	Hamdan al Maktoum

1993

| July Cup | Hamas | Peter Walwyn | Hamdan al Maktoum |

MOST PROLIFIC GROUP 1 WINNERS

5 Salsabil (1989-90)
4 Troy (1979)
  Nashwan (1989)
3 Sun Princess (1983)
  Habibti (1983-84)
  Dayjur (1990)

CARSON'S PATTERN WINNERS OWNED
BY THE QUEEN

1977	**Dunfermline**	Oaks (Gr 1), St Leger (Gr 1)
1979	**Milford**	White Rose Stakes (Gr 3), Princess of Wales's Stakes (Gr 2)
	Expansive	Ribblesdale Stakes (Gr 2)
	Buttress	Queen's Vase (Gr 3)
1980	**Dukedom**	White Rose Stakes (Gr 3)
1982	**Height of Fashion**	Princess of Wales's Stakes (Gr 2)

INDEX

ACKNOWLEDGEMENTS

So long to lay, so quick to hatch. Considering Willie Carson first approached me about this book back at the Lincoln Meeting in 1990, you would have thought there could be no chance of a last minute panic. You would have thought wrong and it is only because of a splendid back-up team that this opus has been able to fly away to bookstalls round the land.

The ubiquitous Jeremy Early stayed up all one night correcting proofs. John Randall is a night owl anyway, but he broke his schedule to update that magnificient battery of Carson statistics. Andrew Wright gave up a fortnight of his vacation to come to my house and grapple with a whole storeful of loose ends. Andrew made the headlines four years ago when he backed himself to get eleven straight 'A's at GCSE. Believe me, this task was much the bigger one.

Marion Paull and her team at Stanley Paul (no apparent relation) have shown patience well beyond the call of duty as has my long-suffering assistant, Cherry Forbes, and my friend and colleague, Paul Hayward, who hung in there with support and belief when various factors put the whole venture in doubt.

But most of all, thanks have to go to the Carson family. To Willie's parents, May and Tommy, who had no doubt long given up any hope of again seeing that large green suitcase of scrapbooks and Carson memorabilia which has spent the last three seasons under my desk. To Elaine, who has always been unfailingly hospitable at any strange time of day or night when I would want to prod her husband into anecdotage.

And finally, thanks to Willie himself. He never wanted to give a syrupy account of the journey he has taken. He bears no responsibility for the comments I have given, some of which he will dispute in his uniquely challenging way. But when he first rang that Doncaster evening, I said that his was a jockey's life that had most to offer the reader, provided it could be directly told. He has honoured his word and my appreciation of his remarkable qualities as well as the odd blemish or two has only increased down the years. He's a whole lot smaller than the famous landmark of his birthplace, but I hope that this book has shown that Stirling has produced something almost to match its castle.

BROUGH SCOTT, August 1993